THE SERMON ON THE MOUNT

THE SERMON ON THE MOUNT

BY
CLOVIS G. CHAPPELL, D.D.

BAKER BOOK HOUSE
Grand Rapids, Michigan

Copyright MCMXXX by Lamar & Whitmore

Copyright renewed 1958 by
Clovis G. Chappell
Reprinted 1975 by
Baker Book House
ISBN: 0-8010-2363-7

PHOTOLITHOPRINTED BY CUSHING - MALLOY, INC.
ANN ARBOR, MICHIGAN, UNITED STATES OF AMERICA
1975

DEDICATED
TO
MR. AND MRS. R. D. HART
WITH AFFECTIONATE
APPRECIATION

CONTENTS

Chapter		Page
I.	POVERTY THAT MAKES RICH	9
II.	BLESSED MOURNERS	22
III.	THE MEEK	35
IV.	A GOOD APPETITE	48
V.	THE MERCIFUL	61
VI.	THE VISION SPLENDID	75
VII.	THE PEACEMAKERS	87
VIII.	THE PERSECUTED	101
IX.	"SALT"	115
X.	LIGHT	128
XI.	FULFILLING THE LAW	140
XII.	DRASTIC OPERATIONS	153
XIII.	THE MOTIVE TEST	166
XIV.	A WISE INVESTMENT	178
XV.	"ASK—SEEK—KNOCK"	191
XVI.	THE WAY OF LIFE	204
XVII.	THE TWO BUILDERS	217

I

POVERTY THAT MAKES RICH

Matthew 5: 3

"Blessed are the poor in spirit: for theirs is the kingdom of heaven."

WHAT an audience this is that faces the Master! The inner circle is made up of his special friends. Beyond them stretch acres of human faces. It is a vast throng. It is made up of all kinds and conditions of men. It is a cross-section of humanity. There are the successful and the failures. There are those who have conquered and those who have been defeated. There are the rich and the poor. There are the literate and the illiterate. They are, doubtless, of varied races and varied religious creeds. In fact, as Jesus speaks to this multitude he is speaking to a miniature world.

But as he looks into their faces, as he looks beyond their faces into their hearts, he sees that they are all out on the same quest. They are all seeking for the same thing. Most of them are seeking blunderingly. They have been disappointed and are doomed to further and deeper disappointment. The pathos of their blind gropings lays hold on the Master's heart. It suggests to him a theme for the sermon of the hour. "Every heart here," he says to himself, "is in search of happiness. But they have missed the way, most of them. I can do nothing better than point out the way that they have missed." Therefore he said: "Blessed are the poor in spirit: for theirs is the kingdom of heaven."

The audience that Jesus faced in that long ago is very close akin to the audience he would face were he to come to our city this morning. The heart of humanity remains unchanged through the years. Were he to stand in Court Square to-day and speak, he would still be moved with compassion as he looked upon the multitude. He would still see them scattered and harassed as sheep without a shepherd. He would still find folks doing a thousand different things in order to be truly happy. He would only find a few who had laid hold on the open secret that is so often hid from the wise and prudent and revealed unto babes. He would take little account of our scientific discoveries and inventions. He would tell us that the roadway to happiness is the same to-day that it was nineteen centuries ago. He would have no better direction to give than that given in our text.

And Jesus can speak with authority about happiness, because it was his constant possession. I am not forgetting that he was a man of sorrows and acquainted with grief. But in spite of that his was the gladdest heart that ever beat in a human bosom. His was the sunniest face that ever looked out on this world. And those who share his poverty of spirit share his happiness. Sorrow may come, but it will only be temporary. "Joy cometh with the

POVERTY THAT MAKES RICH

morning." It is happiness that abides. It is sorrow and sighing that flee away

1

Who are the blessed folks? Who are those that find real happiness?

Jesus makes it plain at once that our happiness is not born of any outward conditions or circumstances. This is a truth that lies right on the surface. It is one that has been established by the experiences of countless millions, yet it seems that every man has to learn it for himself. We still have a feeling that the happy man is the one who achieves outward success. Blessed is the man who makes a fortune. Blessed is he who can write a check in seven figures. Happy is the man who has a palace in the city and a summer palace by the sea or in the mountains. Blessed is the man that has won the applause of his fellows. Blessed is the woman who has become the darling of society. But Jesus says that happiness is not born of what we have.

No more is it born of what we fail to have. When Luke reports this sermon he says: "Blessed are the poor." But poverty is not in itself a blessing. Since it tends to give one a sense of need, it may more readily become a roadway to real happiness than riches. Riches tend to give a false independence. But no man is necessarily blessed simply because he is poor. Nor is any man necessarily unblessed because he is rich. Dives blundered out into the dark. Lazarus found a place in Abraham's bosom. But Dives was not condemned because he was rich, any more than Lazarus was saved because he was poor. One may be just as poor as Lazarus and yet be greedy and grasping and wretched, while another may be as rich as Dives and yet be truly blessed.

When I was a boy there was a rather notorious character in our community who pretended to farm. In reality, however, with the coming of spring the song of Buffalo River cast its spell upon him, and he went fishing practically every day. Now and then, on Saturday afternoons, some farmer who had caught up with his work would go fishing and get Uncle Zeke's fishing place. This gentleman would return from his noon meal to find himself crowded out. Then he would say piously: "You can stay here and fish if you like; I have a family to support." With that he would turn on his heels, go out to the little village, borrow a chew of tobacco, and sit in front of the store and talk theology. And this is what he would say: "Well, I'd rather be a poor man and go to heaven than be a rich man and go to hell." But nobody ever believed that Uncle Zeke was absolutely sure of entrance into the pearly gates simply because he was miserably poor.

Happiness depends not upon what we have, nor upon what we do, but upon what we are. If we seek happiness on the outside, we shall miss it forever. Happiness, if it ever comes, must come from within. It does not depend upon the kind of house in which we live; it depends upon the kind of man

POVERTY THAT MAKES RICH 13

that lives in the house. It does not depend upon the kind of garments in which we dress; it depends upon the kind of individual that is dressed. The kind of man that is happy, said Jesus, is the man that is poor in spirit. He arrives, and he alone.

How utterly ridiculous this must have sounded to some who were listening! How absurd was such a declaration to that Roman, for instance, whose nation had its foot on the neck of the world! How absurd it must have sounded to the Jews who were even more proud than the Roman! It still sounds unbelievable enough even to us. There were those that heard it that day who glanced at each other knowingly, shrugged their shoulders, and swaggered off down the mountain side saying that the Preacher was mad and that there was nothing of real worth in what he was saying. We try to be a little more respectful, yet there are millions to-day who are just as far from believing this statement as the audience to which it was first spoken.

"Blessed are the poor in spirit." "Maybe so," you reply, "yet I cannot work up any enthusiasm for such poverty." But even if you are only half convinced that the poor in spirit are blessed, of one thing you may be sure—that the proud in spirit are unblessed. Here is a truth that not many will deny: Wretched are the proud in spirit. Did you ever see one afflicted with proud flesh? Proud flesh is about the most sensitive something that I know. There is only one thing that is more sensitive and that is a proud spirit. You may be proud of your pride, but of this you may be sure—it is a certain road to wretchedness. Miserable are the proud in spirit. Happy are the poor in spirit.

II

But what does Jesus mean by poverty of spirit? Maybe our lack of enthusiasm for this treasure grows out of our misunderstanding. To be poor in spirit does not mean self-contempt. Jesus never tells us to despise ourselves. He never asks any man to crawl and cringe and grovel. He discovered to us the worth of the individual. He believed that the meanest human soul had immeasurable possibilities, might realize a glorious destiny. To be poor in spirit, therefore, is not to despise yourself. It is not to look upon yourself with contempt. It is to be humble, childlike, teachable, ready to lean upon a higher power.

In order to really understand poverty of spirit it is necessary to see it become incarnate in a personality; otherwise it tends to remain a mere abstraction. The same is true even of so familiar a something as love. I asked a group of little folks sometime ago, "What is love?" and they were utterly silent. I then asked: "Did you ever see any love?" At once every hand went up. They could not define love according to the International Dictionary. Even if they could have done so they would have been little the wiser. But they knew love, none the less. They had seen love become human life. This they had done as they had looked into mother's face

POVERTY THAT MAKES RICH 15

and had felt the kiss of mother's lips and experienced the tender ministry of mother's hands.

Where, then, shall we look for poverty of spirit? Maybe the ten spies will serve as an illustration. They went into Canaan to spy out the land. They came back with a sense of their utter littleness and worthlessness. They declared whimperingly: "We saw the giants that live over there, and we were in our own eyes as grasshoppers. There is no use to undertake to go forward with the enterprise. We can never succeed. God has done nothing more than play a grim joke on us. The whole enterprise is no more than madness." But these men were not poor in spirit; they were poor spirited, and nothing more.

Then we might try the man with one talent. One day he came from his master's presence with a treasure in his hand. That treasure indicated that he was trusted. It showed that his master had confidence in him. He gripped it proudly and thought of the many high adventures that he was going to have with it on the marts of trade. But as he was going to make his first venture he met a friend who had two talents. That dampened his ardor somewhat. Then he met another who had five. After that his zest and ardor went ice cold. He said: "This one little talent is nothing in comparison with what these others have. I will stand no chance at all." So he crept away back home, slunk out into the garden as the shadows gathered, and hid his talent in the earth. But he was not poor in spirit; he was full of pride and fuller still of cowardice.

Where, then, shall we go? Answer: to Jesus himself. These beatitudes are descriptions of the character of our Lord. It is to him, therefore, that we go to find one who in the deepest and fullest sense was poor in spirit. He was so poor in spirit that he said: "I can of mine own self do nothing." He was so poor in spirit that he one day girt himself with a towel and washed the feet of a little handful of men, fishermen and taxgatherers and such like. What a menial task! It was far too mean for any of the disciples. Had I been host that day I might have said to Peter: "Simon, the servants are all out. There is no one here to wash the feet of my guests. You are the leader among them. Suppose you do it." Simon was an excellent man, but he would have bristled and said: "Are you talking to me? You think I am going to wash the feet of Judas and Thomas, of James and John? They are always arguing with me that they are going to be greater than I in the kingdom. If their feet don't get washed till I do it, they will go unwashed forever. Are you trying to insult me?" "No," I might have answered, "I am trying to crown you."

But what none other would do Jesus did. Why? Because he had no respect for himself? No, that was not the reason. Look at the state of his mind as he did this. "Knowing that he was come from God and went to God." That is, when he was conscious of his divine origin, when he was conscious

POVERTY THAT MAKES RICH

that he was going to sit down at the right hand of his Father to receive a name that is above every name, then he girt himself with the towel. Here is true poverty of spirit. Here also is manhood at its best.

III

Why is it that poverty of spirit leads to happiness?

1. It is through poverty of spirit that we come into possession of the kingdom of God. Not that the kingdom is given to us as reward. There is nothing arbitrary about it. "Blessed are the poor in spirit: for theirs is the kingdom of heaven." Such enter naturally, and the door is closed to all others. One day when the disciples were having one of their oft-recurring disputes as to who should be greatest they brought the matter to Jesus. In answer to their question Jesus took a little child and set him in the midst of them and said that the most childlike should be the greatest. Not only so, but that without childlikeness, which is none other than humility or poverty of spirit, it is impossible to enter the kingdom at all. "Except ye be converted, and become as little children, ye shall not enter into the kingdom of heaven."

Jesus told a story of two brothers. The older brother was a steady, hard-working chap who seemed altogether dependable. He kept constantly at home and gave himself with diligence to his duties. But his brother was a waster. He ran away and squandered the wealth his father had given him in riotous living. But though this elder son remained at home and worked, there was never a feast given in his honor. He himself said he had never had so much as a kid with which to make merry with his friends. But one day, as he was returning from the field, he was greeted by the sound of music. He came a little nearer, and the whole household was astir with wildest revelry and joy. Naturally he was concerned to know what was going on. Therefore he called a servant and asked what it meant, and the servant said: "Your brother has come home, and your father has killed for him the fatted calf."

Little wonder that this steady worker was a bit indignant at the turn things had taken! Why did the father show such seeming partiality? It was not that he cared nothing for hard work, but rather set a premium on dissipation. The difference in the treatment of these two sons grew out of what they were in themselves. The elder son reveals himself thoroughly. "Lo, these many years do I serve thee, neither transgressed I at any time thy commandment." That is, he insists that he had never sinned; he had always been perfectly upright. He was, therefore, in no sense poor in spirit. The younger son, on the other hand, had nothing better to say for himself than, "I have sinned against heaven, and before thee, and am no more worthy to be called thy son." The doors of the feast opened

POVERTY THAT MAKES RICH 19

before him automatically, because he was poor in spirit.

2. Then, it is only through poverty of spirit that we remain in the kingdom. Pride certainly goes before destruction, and a haughty spirit before a fall. There is a deal of truth in that classic story of the frog that decided to seek a warmer climate. At first he could think of no fit conveyance in which to go. At last he hit upon this happy contrivance. There were two wild geese that were friends of his. He found a string and asked each one of the geese to take an end. As they did so, he seized the string in the middle. These geese rose into the air, and the frog found himself hurrying toward the land of his dreams. But a spectator from far below, looking up, saw the strange sight and shouted: "Who invented that?" The frog's pride would not allow him to keep silent. He shouted back: "I invented that." But in so doing he let go of the string, and his questioner a moment later was looking upon a bit of minced frog. As in the case of a vast multitude, his pride had been his ruin.

Jesus had a friend who was devoted to him. But this friend was at times a bit proud in spirit. Jesus saw that this was going to undo him, so he undertook to warn him. "All ye shall be offended because of me this night." And Peter took it as personal and denied it flatly. He said: "I cannot speak for these others, James and John and Andrew and the rest. They may fail you, but you can certainly count on me. Though I should die with thee, yet will I not deny thee." And Peter went out in the strength of this confidence to utterly fail. No wonder when he had wept his way back to God he urged his friends to clothe themselves with humility as with a garment. "God resisteth the proud, but gives grace to the humble."

3. Then, poverty of spirit leads to blessedness because it fits us to serve in the kingdom. When the wise man names the six things that God hates, one of them is a proud look. In that we are exactly like him. No one offends us more deeply than the individual who undertakes to lord it over us. It is the man who identifies himself with us, the man of poverty of spirit whose ministry we welcome and find helpful. "Brethren, if a man be overtaken in a fault, ye who are spiritual restore such an one in the spirit of meekness." It is the only way we can restore them. If we go in the spirit of pride, in the spirit of self-sufficiency, we shall repel rather than restore.

F. B. Meyer tells this story: On one occasion he was stopping at a hotel in Norway where there was a little girl who was very fond of playing the piano. But she played only one tune, and played this with just one finger. Naturally she became a bit of a nuisance. When the guests were awakened by her each morning, they would endure it as long as possible, then make their escape as best they could. Now, it so happened that one of the greatest pianists of Norway came that way. He was awakened the next morning along with other guests by this

POVERTY THAT MAKES RICH

tuneless pecking on the piano. He hurriedly dressed and went down into the parlor that the little girl had all to herself. He made himself acquainted with her, told her that he knew the song that she was playing, and asked that he might play it with her. She consented, for she was poor in spirit. He, therefore, took her upon his lap and drowned her discord with his own marvelous melody. And so it may be for ourselves. If in true humility we give first place to the Supreme Master, he will surely touch our heart harp and change its blundering discord into the exquisite music of abiding blessedness.

II

BLESSED MOURNERS

Matthew 5: 4

"Blessed are they that mourn: for they shall be comforted."

WHAT a strange paradox! How flatly it contradicts the accepted views of our day and of every day! Who thinks of congratulating a man because his face is wet with tears? Who thinks of congratulating him because he carries a heavy burden and an aching heart? We pity such. We should no more think of envying a man with tear-blinded eyes than we should think of writing a letter of condolence to some son of good fortune who was managing to get through life without ever receiving a wound or ever struggling under a heavy load. "Blessed are they that mourn," says Jesus. But we cannot agree, so we mark it out and write: "Blessed are the tearless."

But our Lord persists in pronouncing a blessing on the mourners. To his mind the supreme tragedy is that of the tearless eye and the heart without tenderness. You remember how Father Damien went as a missionary to the lepers of far-off Molokai. For thirteen years he shared their Gethsemane. For thirteen years he was their teacher and companion and friend. At last the dread disease laid hold of him. At first he was not aware of it, but one morning he chanced to spill some boiling water on his foot. "How painful!" you say. No, there was not the slightest pain. It was this that told him of his doom. His loss of sensitiveness informed him in language not to be mistaken that death was creeping on him from out the dark.

But there is a far sadder loss than that of physical sensitiveness, even though that loss be the messenger of death. That is the loss of our spiritual sensitiveness. In one of his epistles Paul makes use of a most startling and arresting word. He speaks of certain individuals as being "past feeling." Their sensory nerves had atrophied. They were as incapable of suffering, as completely invulnerable, as the dead. Such loss of feeling indicates something far worse than the death of the body. It indicates the death of the soul. And, mark you, this frightful tragedy was not confined to Paul's day. It has its victims among us who are of the living present.

Yesterday, for instance, you committed a certain sin. But your conscience did not pain you. It did not stuff thorns in your pillow last night when you tried to sleep. That sin had been so persistently repeated that it could now be committed without any pang at all. Recently you heard a sermon that once would have broken your heart. Once such an appeal would have made your very soul leap within you with hope and longing. But to-day it leaves you as unmoved and undisturbed as the pew upon which you sit. Once you could not have passed one who was wounded by the wayside. His suffering would have touched you. You would have bled through his wounds, you would have suffered in his anguish, even though that anguish was of the spirit rather than of the flesh. But now you can look upon the most desperate spiritual need with an indifferent eye.

Some years ago I knew a father of beautiful character and deep devotion. He had a wayward and worthless son. I saw him go to that boy one day and make such an appeal as I have seldom heard. He spilt his hot words of tenderness along with his hot tears upon that son. But the boy seemed neither to hear the words nor feel the tears. He felt the burning yearning and anguish of his father no more than the heroic missionary felt the boiling water upon his foot. But the loss suffered by the wayward boy was infinitely greater than that suffered by the missionary.

"Blessed are they that mourn." Of course Jesus does not mean that every mourner is necessarily blessed. Tears are not good in and of themselves. There are tears, thank God, that seem to wash bright the eyes and spread beauty on the cheeks as they flow. They seem to water the gardens of the heart and set the fields of the soul to flowering. But there are other tears that leave the eyes smarting and blinded. They fret channels upon the cheeks and scorch and wither the verdure of the heart. There are, then, mourners whose mourning brings them no comfort. There are others whose

BLESSED MOURNERS

mourning is the open roadway to heavenly consolation.

I

Among those mourners whose mourning leaves them without comfort we may mention the following:

1. The deliberate pessimist. There are those who are veritable gluttons for wretchedness. They search for despair as bees search for honey. They are never so happy as when they feel that they have a perfect right to be miserable. They are never so miserable as when they feel duty bound to be happy. They make Paul's beautiful words read like this: "Finally, brethren, whatsoever things are false, whatsoever things are dishonest, whatsoever things are unjust, whatsoever things are impure, whatsoever things are unlovely, whatsoever things are of evil report, if there be any vice, and if there be any condemnation, think on these things." So they think, and so thinking mourn, but their mourning brings no comfort.

2. Neither is one necessarily blessed for mourning over some selfish loss or thwarted ambition. I knew a man years ago who seemed to have a veritable passion for popularity. He was keenly ambitious to lead. But his plans went awry, and I cannot but think of him to-day as a most unhappy man. But his mourning brings him no consolation. It would be hard to find a more tragic mourner than Napoleon in his lonely exile. His crown had been

snatched from his brow, his scepter wrenched from his hands. But his mourning was not the pathway to blessedness. What a mourner was Dean Swift! "It is awful," says Thackeray, "to think of the great suffering of this great man. . . . As fierce a beak and talon as ever struck, . . . as strong a wing as ever beat belonged to Swift. I am glad, for one, that fate wrested the prey out of his claws, and cut his wings and chained him. One can gaze, not without awe and pity, at the lonely eagle chained behind the bars." A pathetic mourner, indeed, but one without comfort.

3. Not even are those necessarily blessed who have suffered the loss of some loved one. Of course such loss has been the roadway to comfort for multitudes. Elisha was never the same after he had seen Elijah go home. You have not been the same since your baby died. You have had a different feeling about God, about the reality of the unseen, since you kneeled by the coffin of your mother. But even this kind of loss does not always bring blessed results. I recall a mother who belonged to my church in another city. This mother lost her boy. But she was not made soft and tender by her sorrow. She was made hard and bitter and rebellious. If I were out searching for one of the most miserable beings in all the world, I should certainly knock at her door.

4. Nor are those blessed whose mourning is born of remorse. There are many sinners who mourn, but their mourning is not always born of any hatred

BLESSED MOURNERS 27

of sin. They do not hate evil, they hate its effects. Our jails and penitentiaries are full of people who mourn, but their mourning does not always bring them comfort. Jesus tells us that hell is full of mourners, people who weep and wail; but their tears bring no blessing, and their sorrow is without consolation. Therefore it is possible to mourn, and mourn deeply, and yet find no benediction.

II

Who, then, are those whose mourning ends in comfort?

Speaking broadly, this is true of every one whose mourning leads to Jesus Christ. Whatever your sorrow, whatever your burden, whatever your heartache, if it turns your blundering steps toward him, you are sure to find consolation and comfort. How many could testify to the truth of this! Some of you could stand in your places even now and tell how the blackest days of your lives became, through the riches of his grace, roadways into the brightest of mornings. The very thing that you thought would work your ruin has been your remaking. The rough path of yesterday that seemed all thorns and jagged rocks has become strangely smooth under your weary feet. You would not now exchange your bitterest sorrow for the world's rarest joy. This is true because it was through that desperate night of agony that you were led to seek and to find Jesus.

But the mourning that the Master especially has

in mind is mourning over sin. This beatitude follows naturally upon the heels of the one preceding. "Blessed are the poor in spirit," Jesus said in the first. Blessed is the man who is conscious that he is not what he should be. Blessed is the man with a sense of need, the man who realizes that he can of himself do nothing. But our beatitude goes further. Blessed is the man who is not only conscious of his failure, but who grieves over it, who takes it to heart. Blessed is the man who is so grieved over his moral and spiritual lack that he turns his face toward Him who is able to supply his need.

The knowledge of our spiritual poverty would be of little worth unless it led to mourning. It would avail little for the prodigal to realize that he was away in the far country by the swine trough should such realization bring him no grief. It would count for nothing for him to be conscious of his hunger if he should content himself with the husks that the swine did eat. The tragedy of his plight must strike home to his heart. He must be so tortured by it that he will loathe the thing that he is. He must be so tortured that he will resolve to rise and go to his father. So often our poverty is without a pang. So often our very confessions of sin are cold and formal. They do not burst from us hot with shame and wet with tears. Too few care enough to mourn. Therefore we do not find the consolation and the strength promised in our text.

Not only are those blessed who mourn for their

own sins, but there is blessing and comfort for those who mourn over the sins of others. Jesus was this kind of mourner. Let us remember that these beatitudes, while partially describing the children of the kingdom, far more accurately describe the character of the Master himself. "Himself took our infirmities, and bare our sorrows." Blessed, therefore, is the man that shares with Jesus the pain and anguish of a world gone wrong. Blessed is the man who enters into the fellowship of his suffering. Blessed is he that fills up that which is lacking of the suffering of Christ in his own body. Blessed is he who struggles under the weight of another's woe, who cries: "I will gladly spend and be spent for you; though the more I love, the less I be loved."

III

What is the natural outcome of such mourning? Those who so mourn are comforted. They are strengthened and consoled.

1. That is true of those who mourn because of their own sin. The outcome of such mourning is reconciliation with God. It ends in pardon and peace that passeth all understanding. Here, for instance, is a young man in great anguish. "Woe is me," he cries desperately, "for I am undone. I am a man of unclean lips." The careless world looks on with amazement and pity. "Why does he take things so hard? Why does he not throw it off and forget about it?" But do not pity him. He is on the threshold of a great discovery. He is entering

upon a new day. For a live coal is laid upon his lips, and a voice whispers: "Lo, this has touched thy lips, and thine iniquity is taken away, and thy sin purged." His mourning was the gateway to comfort.

Here is another miserable creature whose agony is utterly amazing. He is not a weak man; he is one of the world's strong men. Yet the tragic cry that is wrung from him by his pain makes us shudder after all these centuries. "O wretched man that I am! who shall deliver me?" "Poor fellow," one says, "he is too sensitive." But again I say, dare not pity him. He is on the point of entering upon a new world. "Who shall deliver me?" He cries desperately: "God will and does. He does it through Jesus Christ. 'There is therefore now no condemnation to them that are in Christ Jesus.'"

But, mark you, this mourning must be mourning for sin and not simply for its consequences. There are two outstanding sinners in the Old Testament whose paths cross. One is Saul, the other is David. Saul sinned and sinned deeply, though not so deeply as David. Saul confessed his sin, too. He confessed more often than any other man in the Bible. Saul was a mourner. But he never mourned except for the evil plight into which his sin brought him. He never learned to hate sin itself. He never confessed his sin except when he was in a tight corner and there seemed no other way of escape except through confession. Therefore he died uncomforted and unblessed.

But with David it was different. What a desperate sinner he was, and how he suffered! His moisture was turned into drought of summer. The garden of his heart became a burning desert. At last he burst into God's presence and threw himself at his feet and prayed: "Have mercy upon me, O God, according to thy loving-kindness: according to the multitude of thy tender mercies blot out my transgressions." "Create in me a clean heart, O God. Deliver me from bloodguiltiness." His heart is broken over his sin. And what is the outcome? His sobbing is changed into song. "Blessed is he whose transgression is forgiven, whose sin is covered."

There are also two outstanding sinners in the New Testament whose paths cross. They are Peter and Judas. Peter through cowardice committed a sin close akin to that of Judas. But when Peter realized the wound that he had inflicted upon the Master whom he loved and who loved him, it broke his heart. He wept his way back to the cross. Jesus could hardly wait till he had got the door of his tomb open before he gave Peter a private interview. After that he trusted him with the delicate task of feeding his lambs and being the shepherd of his sheep. Judas also mourned. But there was no grief for wounded love in his tears. Therefore his mourning brought him nothing better than a hangman's noose and a grave in the potter's field.

Then there is comfort and consolation for those who mourn over the sins of others. This is the case, not because such mourning is cheap; it is very costly. The tears of Jesus were not shallow tears. He beheld the city and wept over it, but he did more than weep. He went down to cleanse its temple. He went down to plead with its crowds. He went down to die for its heedless and hating multitudes. And if we mourn as Jesus our grief must not be the shallow grief of the votary of the movies who wipes his eyes that have grown wet over some imaginary sorrow that he forgets as soon as the show is over. It must be a grief that sends us out to share with Jesus in his efforts to save the world.

Paul was a mourner after this fashion. What burdens he carried, and how gladly he carried them! He speaks again and again of his tears. He tells us that he has suffered the loss of all things. He knew the inside of numerous Roman prisons. There was scarcely a square inch of his body that did not bear a scar. He was always giving himself eagerly, gladly. His life was a daily dying. He writes out "of much affliction and anguish of heart." In his solicitude for others he has "great heaviness and continual sorrow." He has a passion to save that will give him no rest.

But, so burdened, is he not miserable? No, strange to say, he is the most joyful of men. The lilt of his song rings with amazing sweetness and gladness through prison cells. Though he is writing in great anguish of heart and with tears, even in the midst of these tears he cannot repress a shout of genuine gladness. "Blessed be God, even the

BLESSED MOURNERS 33

Father of our Lord Jesus Christ, the Father of mercies, and the God of all comfort; who comforteth us in all our tribulation. . . . For as the sufferings of Christ abound in us, so our consolation also aboundeth by Christ." "The greater the mourning," says Paul, "the greater the comfort." It is perfectly natural that it should be so. The more we mourn after this fashion, the more dead we become to self. The more dead we become to self, the more alive we become to God. It is when self dies under the stroke of the cross that we can truly sing:

> "Only the sorrows of others
> Cast a shadow over me."

It is then that we enter most fully into the comfort which Jesus promises in our text.

Those who enter into the fellowship of Christ's suffering do find comfort. They find it not only by and by, but here and now. They find it in all circumstances, in all situations. Here, for instance, is a man clinging to a bit of wreckage in an icy sea. The Titanic upon which he was a passenger has just gone down. His freezing fingers can with difficulty keep their grip upon all that holds him from death amidst the creeping things at the bottom of the ocean. But there is no panic. He is strangely at leisure from himself. Therefore, when another bit of wreckage floats by in the dim twilight of the early morning, he thinks only of the needs of the man he sees clinging to it. He calls to him: "Young man, are you saved?" "No," comes the answer. "Believe on the Lord Jesus Christ, and thou shalt be saved." And the young man then and there believed. He lived to tell the story. But the man that flung open the door of life to him lost his hold a moment later and was seen no more. But surely he knew through his own experience in that testing hour that God does give comfort to those who mourn. There was a Presence with him more real than death, a Presence that made the unstable waters to become the very Rock of Ages under his feet, that made the bit of wreckage to which he clung the threshold of his Father's house.

III

THE MEEK

Matthew 5: 5

"Blessed are the meek: for they shall inherit the earth."

I

This beatitude is by no means popular. To the man of the world it makes the least possible appeal. In truth, I think it safe to say that it makes no appeal at all. This is true for at least two reasons.

1. Meekness is not looked upon by him as an asset. He regards it rather as a liability. He is by no means convinced that the meek are really blessed. He is not at all sure that they are to be congratulated. He thinks it possible that they are to be despised. He feels at times that they might well be looked on with contempt. Occasionally they are to be pitied. But surely they are not to be looked upon as having come into possession of a truly worthful treasure. Who really desires to be meek? Most of us would be ashamed of such a virtue. We regard meekness as little better than a synonym for weakness. A newspaper spoke recently of a certain man who had assisted his dominant paramour in the killing of her husband as "a meek little murderer."

2. Then, the man of the world objects to this text because he does not believe it true that the meek

shall inherit the earth. In fact, he feels that there is no group that is less likely to inherit the earth than the meek. He is ready enough to believe that they will go to heaven when they die; but as for inheriting the earth in the life that now is, nothing could be farther from the truth. He believes in the survival of the fittest. He believes the most fit to survive in a world like ours is the aggressive, heavy-handed, hard-fisted, self-assertive man. What chance has the meek in a world where it seems so evident that the race is always to the swift, and the battle to the strong?

Now, there is no shutting our eyes to the fact that this position seems quite sane. It seems shot through with an abundance of good common sense. "Blessed are the meek; for they shall inherit the earth." How ridiculous that would look if it were framed and hung as a motto in many a business office! How out of place it would sound to many, if heard amidst the busy rush of our city streets or the loud hum of our factories. Yet it would certainly sound no more ridiculous to us than it did to those to whom it was first spoken. It seemed little less than madness then. Yet Jesus believed in the truthfulness of it and said so with conviction. Were he to come amidst the hustle and push of our modern life, he would still say with calm and quiet confidence: "Blessed are the meek: for they shall inherit the earth." And we, sad to say, would be almost as far from believing him as was the multitude on the

THE MEEK

mountain side. There are still all too few who look upon this beatitude with appreciation and confidence.

II

But if meekness seems small and worthless to many of ourselves, there is no shutting our eyes to the fact that this was not the case with those saints whom we meet upon the pages of the Bible. It is especially not the case with the writers of the New Testament. Take Paul for example. No cowardly weakling was he. He was one of the most dauntless of men. He admired those virtues that are virile and masterly. He declared proudly: "We Christians are not cowards." He rejoiced that God has not given us a spirit of fearfulness, but of power and of love and of a sound mind. No one would have been further than he from urging his friends to seek a cheap and flimsy virtue. But one day he wrote a letter to Timothy, his own son in the faith. Timothy, you remember, was a young man who really never succeeded in growing up. He was sickly. He was timid and retiring. Yet Paul urges this timid youth to "follow after meekness." He is to pursue it. He is never to rest satisfied till he had enriched his spiritual life by the possession of this priceless virtue.

On another occasion this same author is writing to his converts at Colosse. He is telling them how to dress in a fashion becoming the sons and daughters of the King. He is instructing them how they are to clothe themselves so as to vastly enhance their charm and usefulness. Therefore he writes this wise word: "Put on . . . meekness." It was his conviction that one garbed in this fine fashion would be equipped both for the life that now is and for that which is to come.

Again, in his letter to the Galatians Paul is telling us of some of the rare and winsome flowers that the Heavenly Gardener plants in the garden of the soul when he is allowed to have his way. "The fruit of the Spirit is love, joy, peace, long-suffering, gentleness, goodness, faithfulness, meekness." Meekness, then, is a fruit of the Spirit. It is a virtue so priceless, so altogether winsome that we cannot attain it in the energy of the flesh. It must come to us, if at all, through the power of the Spirit. It is, therefore, very evident that this aggressive, clear-thinking, and Christlike saint was convinced that meekness is not a liability, but a most worthful and beautiful asset.

A glance at the letters of Peter indicates that he was of the same opinion. In his first epistle he says: "Whose adorning let it not be outward, . . . but let it be the hidden man of the heart, . . . even the ornament of a meek and quiet spirit, which is in the sight of God of great price." He is aware of the fact that meekness often fails to look well in the eyes of men. He knows that we have a tendency to despise it, to regard it as utterly worthless. But it is not so looked upon by Him who sees things clearly and sees them whole. We often mistake the worthful for the worthless, and the worthless for the worthful. Often we mistake tinsel for fine gold, and gold for

THE MEEK 39

tinsel. We count of high value what God despises, and despises what He sees to be of abiding worth.

Years ago, we are told, there was a peddler who pushed a cart about the back streets of Paris earning a meager living by selling cheap jewelry and trifling gewgaws. Among his commonplace wares there was a bit of stone tagged with a dirty little card that bore this inscription; "Rock crystal, price twenty-four francs." It seemed for a long time that nobody wanted this piece of rock crystal. Of course the price was rather high for an object of such seemingly small value. But one day a man chanced to pass that way who had a seeing eye. He had ability to distinguish the worthless from the worthful, the best from the second best. He saw value in this bit of rock crystal that other eyes failed to see. In fact, he saw that it was not rock crystal at all, but genuine diamond. So he bought it, and that rare gem is now said to be among the royal jewels of a great nation. In the same fashion many tend to pass by the rare gem of meekness, while only the few realize its value and seek to possess it.

Then, when we ask what men of the Bible are the most conspicuous for their meekness, what do we find? For instance, who is the outstanding example of meekness in the Old Testament? He is not some despised weakling, he is not some nameless craven. The supreme example of meekness in the Old Testament is Moses. And what a superb man he is! He is a lawgiver of the highest order. He is a prophet. He is the builder of a nation. In fact, he is one of the genuinely great men of all time.

When we turn to the New Testament we find that the supreme example of meekness is none other than Jesus himself. When the evangelists tell of his entrance into Jerusalem, it is his meekness that they emphasize. Paul, writing to the Corinthians, beseeches them by the gentleness and meekness of Jesus. Even Jesus himself calls our attention to his possession of this fine virtue. "Learn of me," he says. And when he makes this appeal he does not base it upon his possession of wisdom, though in him are hidden all the treasures of wisdom and knowledge. But he says, rather: "Learn of me; for I am meek and lowly of heart." Meekness is his outstanding characteristic. It is the one virtue in himself to which he calls our attention. It is that which he seems most to desire us to imitate. Therefore we are safe in concluding that meekness is a virtue of real worth. Whatever makes us more like Moses, especially whatever makes us more like Jesus, will not impoverish, but will surely enrich us.

III

What is meekness? It is a word that is a bit difficult to define. One reason for this is that it has largely gone out of use. We do not employ it very often in our ordinary conversation. To some, therefore, it has almost no meaning at all, while to other it has a meaning that is inadequate, if not altogether erroneous. There are those, for instance, who think of the meek man as a rather spineless creature, gifted by nature with a sweet temper and a quick readiness to bow before every breeze. He is, therefore, to be tolerated only because he never takes a stand on any question, nor ever dares to get in anybody's way. But nothing could be further from the truth. What a hot-tempered man is Moses when we first meet him! He could strike a fellow being dead in his blazing anger without the slightest compunction. Yet he became the meekest of men. Meekness is, therefore, something far different from being merely good natured. It is far different from weakness. It is strength grown tender. It is might with a caress in its brawny hands. There is a word that is used in connection with meekness more than once. That word is "gentle." "The servant of the Lord must not strive, but be gentle, patient, apt to teach, in meekness instructing those that oppose themselves." Again: "Put them in mind, . . . that they be no brawlers, but gentle, showing all meekness to all men." That is, the meek folks are the gentle folks; the meek man is Christ's real gentleman.

Now, what are some of the characteristics of this Christian gentleman? Mark you, I am not describing what the world calls a gentleman. I am not undertaking to give the characteristics of the man who is commonly styled a gentleman in the social sense. I am not talking about him who is a gentleman by accident of gentle birth. I am talking about the man who is a gentleman by spiritual birth, the man who has come to possess, in some measure, the meekness and gentleness of Jesus. I am, therefore, talking about the highest type of gentleman.

> "Kind hearts are more than coronets,
> And simple faith than Norman blood."

1. This Christian gentleman is considerate of others. He does not insist upon having the best for himself. He does not elbow women and children out of the way in order to get on a street car first. He does not turn two seats together on the train while a woman with a crying baby in her arms is compelled to stand. He does not seek to push others to the rear of the procession in the rush of life. He is thoughtful of others. He is genuinely courteous. He never inflicts a needless wound. He lightens his brother's burden when he has opportunity. He gives to all men something of the fine consideration that was accorded by Jesus himself.

2. This gentleman has a sweet temper. He does not give himself the luxury of flying into a rage and speaking his mind. Now, I am aware of the fact that bad temper is not generally looked upon with very great disapproval. In fact, there are those who rather pride themselves on being quick to blaze and to let themselves go. But I think that Drummond was probably right in saying that bad temper causes more real suffering than almost any other one sin. This Christian gentleman refrains from anger, not because he has no temper, but because he controls his temper by the grace of God.

THE MEEK

3. This gentleman is humble-minded. He does not swagger. He does not boast over his possessions or over his achievements. He does not see fit to be everlastingly informing the world about how good he is, or how much he has suffered, or how many crosses he bears for others. He has the child heart. He is teachable. He is ready to take the lowest place. He is so thoughtful of others that he forgets himself. He is Christlike in his humility.

4. This gentleman is courageous. He has the highest type of courage. He dares a terror before which many of the most lion-hearted quail. What do men fear most? It is not pain, nor death, nor sin. There is nothing of which the average man is more horribly afraid than of being thought a coward. We are ready to face almost any danger rather than that dread foe. But the meek man is so courageous that he dares look that terrible enemy in the face with quiet eyes. This he does because he longs, above all else, to be like Him who, "when he was reviled, reviled not again."

5. Christ's gentleman is strong. The gentle things are ever the strong things. Gravitation does not make any great noise, but how mighty it is! When Elijah stood in the mouth of his cave an earthquake shook the mountain. That suited the temper of the prophet. That was his idea of what God ought to do for the sinful of the world. But he discovered that God was not in the earthquake. He discovered, further, that he was neither in the roaring tempest, nor in the raging fire. He was rather in the voice

small and still. There are people yet who fancy that the power is in the thunder rather than in the lightning. But noise is not necessarily strong. It may be very weak. More than once have I heard loud talking and loud swearing made into a kind of smoke screen behind which some coward was seeking to hide his weakness. It is gentleness that is strong.

How did it come about that those money changers in the temple ran so readily at the approach of Jesus? Why did they not resist him? Why did they not hold their ground and defy him? Why did they not challenge his authority and demand that he show his credentials? They were not all cowards. Besides, their interests were at stake. To have their tables overturned and their business interfered with was both annoying and costly. Yet they fled wildly without counting the cost. Why was this the case? It would never have happened if Jesus had been no more than a mere dictatorial blusterer. That which made his anger so terrible was that it was the anger of the meek. That which made his wrath so irresistible was that it was "the wrath of the Lamb."

IV

Now, the text tells us that the blessing promised to the meek is that they shall inherit the earth. This, you know, is a quotation from the thirty-seventh Psalm. Jesus did not originate this word, but he read it and memorized it and believed it with all his heart. He believed it because it is true.

1. It is true literally. If we believe our Bibles, we believe that there is coming a day when Jesus is going to reign "from the rivers to the ends of the earth." We believe that the glory of God is one day going to cover the earth as the waters cover the sea. We believe that in spite of the seeming eternity and prosperity of wrong it is righteousness that is going to abide and to be finally triumphant. We believe that when Jesus taught us to pray, "Thy kingdom come," he was not teaching us to dream dreams that could never come true. He was teaching us to pray for that which is one day sure to be realized. And when that day comes there will not be a man in all the world who is not meek. When that day comes every man will be a gentleman.

2. Then, the meek are already entering upon their inheritance. They are coming more and more to possess the earth with the passing of the centuries. We recognize this fact among the lower orders of life. There certainly ought to be more eagles and hawks and owls than sparrows and doves and catbirds. What chance have these latter little creatures against the fierce beak and talons of the birds of prey? But, strange to say, it is the birds of prey that are being slowly exterminated, while those that are defenseless continue to multiply. The lion and the tiger certainly ought to have a better chance in a world like ours than the lamb. Yet for every lion and for every tiger there are millions of

lambs. Among the lower orders of life it is the meek that are inheriting the earth.

The same is true among the nations. It certainly seems that the warlike nations ought to be counted on to inherit the earth. But history flatly contradicts this assumption. There have been all too many nations in the past that were little more than beasts of prey. They ground the weak beneath their heels and grew rich and mighty through the shedding of blood. But where are they now? They have passed into the graveyárd of buried nations. They died of their own conquests. They got themselves exterminated, committed actual suicide, in a mad and futile effort to possess the earth. The nation in any age that seeks by force to inherit the earth is certainly doomed. This is as true of the self-seeking nation of to-day, if it continues its course, as it is of those dead nations whose dust already litters up the roadways of the centuries.

3. The meek inherit the earth in the finest and truest sense in the here and now. For, to inherit the earth, it is not necessary that one literally possess it. Those inherit it who find in it the richest and fullest and freest life. The selfish man cannot inherit the earth. The small bit of the earth that he wins rather possesses him and makes him, in some measure, its slave, while the wealth that is not his tends to make him restless by exciting his desire or his envy. But with the meek it is different. I have an old friend who recently spent a day sight-seing in New York City. He had a delightful time. But

when he returned to his hotel, he bowed reverently before God and said: "Lord, I just want to thank thee that I haven't seen a thing to-day that I want." This man is inheriting the earth. He can admire without coveting, and enjoy without owning.

Then, the meek live the fullest and richest life because they are the most capable of giving. Paul was wise when he told Timothy to use meekness in his instruction. We enjoy being instructed by the meek, but if the proud and boastful swaggerer seeks to instruct us we resent it. He was wise in instructing that we restore the erring in the spirit of meekness. The true Christian gentleman can so rebuke as to soften and win us back to God. But the man who is proud and arrogant embitters and alienates. Therefore, in the here and now, the meek, in the fullest and finest sense, are inheriting the earth.

"We live in deeds, not years; in thoughts, not breaths;
In feelings, not in figures on a dial.
We should count time by heart throbs when they beat
For God, for man, for duty.
He most lives who thinks most, feels the noblest, acts the best."

IV

A GOOD APPETITE

Matthew 5: 6

"Blessed are they which do hunger and thirst after righteousness: for they shall be filled."

I

EVERYBODY recognizes the fact that a good appetite is a bit of a treasure. That is, everybody with the possible exception of some one who has never lost his appetite. If you have always gone eagerly and gladly to three square meals a day, if you have always been able to eat whatever you wished and whenever you wished it, then, possibly, your appreciation will be small. But, on the other hand, if you have known what it is to lose your appetite, if you have passed through long, lean, gray months when the very odor of food was repellent and the taste of the most palatable of dishes nauseated, then you know at least in some measure how to appreciate a good appetite and are ready to agree that those who hunger and thirst, even in the realm of the physical, are to be congratulated. A good appetite is a blessing for the following reasons:

1. It is a mark of life. Living things hunger and thirst. That tree out yonder is hungering and thirsting every moment. This is true for the simple

A GOOD APPETITE 49

reason that it is alive. An ordinary beech tree will drink sixty-five gallons on a hot summer day. An oak tree will drink far more. Some of this water must be carried to a height of more than one hundred feet. How this is done, nobody knows. But the tree lifts it in some way because it is so thirsty. When a tree ceases to hunger and thirst it will die. Or, to speak more correctly, it is already dead. The living hunger. Only the dead are absolutely without appetite. I officiated sometime ago at the funeral of a Chinaman. When the services were over a friend of the deceased came forward and put a bottle of water and a bit of bread into the casket. This was to serve the departed on his journey into the unknown. But the gift was received without the slightest appreciation. The dead man showed no gratitude whatsoever. He had ceased altogether to hunger and thirst.

2. Not only is a good appetite a mark of life, but it is a mark of normal and vigorous and healthful life. Hunger and thirst are perfectly normal. The other day you went to see your physician. You were below par for some reason. So you consulted an expert in the matter of health. The doctor questioned you about your symptoms. Among the questions that he asked was this: "How is your appetite?" He knew that if you did not hunger and thirst something was wrong with you. Loss of appetite is the red flag that nature hangs out to tell us that there is danger ahead. Happy, therefore, is the man who has a good appetite.

3. Then, a good appetite is a roadway to growth. That little baby in the cradle is a bundle of hungers and thirsts. He does not know for what he is hungering and thirsting, but he knows when he gets it. Not only so, but he compels the whole household to know if he does not get it. That is as it should be. Just so long as he keeps a good appetite will he grow, but if he ceases to hunger and thirst he will cease to grow. He will fail to reach his highest physical possibilities. If one has already reached maturity, hunger and thirst are needful in order to keep the body in repair. Our cars can no more run without gasoline than our bodies without food and drink. There is a sense in which we die daily. This death must be constantly repaired by wholesome eating and drinking, or our physical machinery will become mere wreckage.

4. Then, incidentally, a good appetite is a blessing because it is a source of genuine enjoyment. We are fond of speaking of the bread that mother used to make. Excellent bread it must have been, but I am not at all sure that it was any better than the bread we have to-day. We only had better appetites then. A good appetite is certainly the most essential factor in the enjoyment of a dinner. It is a delight to eat when one is genuinely hungry. It is a delight to feed a hungry man, as every housewife will testify. But it is next to impossible to feed one that is not hungry. More than one faithful wife has grown gray before her time in an effort

to coax the lagging appetite of some dyspeptic husband whose every meal was a bore.

II

But there are other hungers than the hunger for bread. Man must have bread. He cannot live without it. But while bread is essential, it is not enough. "Man shall not live by bread alone." His hunger for bread is very real. This hunger he shares along with the lower orders of life. In addition, however, to this hunger he has higher hungers that are the badge of his superiority. When I was a boy on the farm I owned a faithful dog named Jack. Jack and I were the best and most intimate of friends. I have never loved any other dog as I loved him. Many a meal have I shared with him. I would give him of my bread and meat ungrudgingly. At times I would even give him a bit of cake, if I could spare it. Having eaten together, we often went together and drank out of the same gurgling spring. His appetite was quite as keen as mine. His enjoyment of his eating and drinking seemed quite as great as mine. But having left the dinner table, we parted company. I had hungers and thirsts to which he was an absolute stranger.

For instance, I would sometimes look at the range of majestic hills that encircled our farm and wonder what lay beyond. "What a wonderful world that must be over there!" I would say to myself. "Some day I am going to see that world. I am going to mix with it and become a part of it." As other normal boys, I would now and then feel

"The wild pulsation that we feel before the strife,
  When we hear our days before us and the tumult of our life."

But Jack never shared my dreams. He knew nothing of my eagerness to see the big world that lay beyond the hills. I early learned to love some of the musical passages in the King James Version of the Bible. But, when I quoted the twenty-third Psalm or the fourteenth chapter of St. John, Jack was not even mildly interested. I liked songful poetry, even when I did not understand it. But the reading of the most tender and tuneful songs failed utterly to win his interest. Sometimes in sorrow for sin, or under the spell of a longing to be better, I would pray. But all this was beyond the comprehension of my dog. He never thrilled at the splendor of a sunrise, never paused to listen to the song of a mocking bird. We could share a piece of bread with mutual enjoyment, but the music that thrilled and delighted me only made him howl.

Now, these higher hungers belong in a larger or lesser degree to every one of us. They are a badge, I repeat, of our superiority. They are a mark of our greatness. They are the secret of our progress, intellectually and spiritually. Take the hunger to know, for example. How much we owe to the men who have possessed an insatiable hunger for knowledge! How much we are indebted to those who determined

> "To follow knowledge like a sinking star,
> Beyond the utmost bounds of human thought!"

These have been the teachers of the race. They have brought to us all our inventions. They have been the great explorers and discoverers. Their hands have mapped the continents. They have also mapped the heavens as well. Blessed is he of the hungry mind. Blessed is he who longs to know. He shall find in some measure for himself and, possibly in finding, become a teacher of others.

But man has not been and cannot be content with the knowledge of things. He has not been satisfied with the exploring of the little world on which he lives, nor even with his partial exploration of the universe. He is hungry to know Him who is the Creator of it all. He is thirsty for the knowledge of him

> "Whose dwelling is the light of setting suns,
> And the round ocean, and the living air,
> And the blue sky, and in the mind of man."

God has placed in every one of us an insatiable hunger for himself. Therefore when the Psalmist says,

> "As the hart panteth after the water brooks,
> So panteth my soul after thee, O God,"

he is speaking a universal language. When Philip says, "Lord, show us the Father, and it is enough," he is voicing a longing that is as old as man, and that is the very mother of religion.

But while the hunger for God is a universal hunger, the tragedy is that so often we misunderstand our own longings. We do not know that for which we hunger. Hence we pursue many false trails. We attain many vain goals that, when attained, leave the lips still parched and the heart still unsatisfied. The secret of a great part of the fret and restlessness and fitful feverishness of our world today grows out of the fact that it is a hungry world and is failing to find that for which it hungers. In our desperation we often so persistently cultivate an appetite for the second best, or even for the worst, that we allow our higher hungers to become dormant and, for all practical purposes, utterly dead.

As a proof of this, consider the vast number of people who frankly have no taste for the spiritual. The most inspiring service ever held would scarcely awaken their interest. The best sermon ever preached would bore them. The very thought of worship is repellent. The Bible, throbbing with "thoughts that breathe and words that burn," is to them the deadest of dead books. The great hymns of the Church, that for centuries have thrilled the hungry hearts of devout men and women and have served as stairways by which they have climbed into the presence of God, leave them dull and listless and uninterested. The man who has lost all appetite for his daily bread is to be pitied, but how infinitely greater is the tragedy when we lose all desire for the Bread of Life! It is by no means difficult to find those who have so long and so persist-

A GOOD APPETITE

ently fed upon the leeks and garlic of Egypt that they seem to have lost all taste for the heavenly manna.

I was reading not long ago of a certain man who took a street car in an effort to attend a Sunday baseball game. In some way he got on the wrong car. He found himself, to his utter consternation, surrounded by a group of pious people who were on their way to a revival meeting. There was much spiritual fervor among them. They that feared the Lord were speaking one with another, and this gentleman found himself rubbing elbows with two old saints who were telling what the Lord had done for them. He knew at once he was in the wrong pew. He was embarrassed and distressed. He rang the bell and hastened to get off at the next corner. Having made his escape, he sought the right car and at last found himself among companions more congenial. He told them about the distressing predicament from which he had just extricated himself. He described it in these fitting words: "I found myself between two old prayer meeting saints, and I was certainly in one hell of a fix." There you have it. What was heaven to the saints was hell to him. He had no taste for such things.

Such was the case of the man with the muck rake of whom Bunyan tells. He was a very busy man. His eyes were fixed upon the earth where he was diligently raking up some muck and sticks and straw. Meanwhile an angel was poised above his head with a crown waiting to crown him if he would only look up. But he had no interest in the higher things. Such was the case with the crane that was picking up snails on the muddy bank of a muddy pond. A swan lighted at his side. "Where are you from?" asked the crane. "From heaven," was the answer. And the swan began to describe the glories of that heavenly home. But the crane was not interested. He broke in for one question: "Are there any snails there?" When the swan answered in the negative, the crane would not listen for a moment longer. He simply had no taste for the beauties of which the swan spoke. Even so we lose our appetite for those higher values that outlast the ages.

III

But there are some who have not suffered this sad loss. Blessed, therefore, is he who hungers and thirsts after righteousness.

What is this righteousness that we are to desire? It is more than justice. It is more than fair play. It is goodness. Good is not a thrilling word in our day. It leaves us rather pulseless. Yet, when it becomes flesh and blood and walks among us, it is about the most gripping and winsome something that I know. Luke says of Barnabas that he was a good man. If we, therefore, get acquainted with Barnabas, we shall have some idea of goodness. What manner of man was Barnabas? Was he a man that one can truly admire? Was he a man that one would be glad to have as a friend? Was he one whose presence would be a delight? Would he be a genuine inspiration and benediction to any circle in which he might move?

When we come to know him we must confess that such was the case.

1. He was beautifully generous. He was always ready to believe the best. When Paul, who had recently been the scourge of the Church, came to Jerusalem claiming to have been converted, nobody believed him. Yes, there was one radiant exception, and that was this good man Barnabas. He stood by him and stood for him and saved him to the Church. When John Mark turned coward and deserted and went home, Paul refused to give him a second chance. But Barnabas was different. He could not give him up, even though he had failed and failed miserably. He clung to him till Paul acknowledged the victory of his generosity and wrote, "Bring Mark, for he is profitable unto me for the ministry." He looked for the best, not simply among his own people, but among others as well. When he came down to Antioch, where some who were not Jews were being won to Christianity, he was quick to recognize them as fellow Christians. He thanked God for them and entered heartily with them into the work. He was generous in his judgments, and equally so in the use of his wealth. He laid all that he possessed upon the altar of his Lord.

Then, he was a source of consolation. He was incarnate encouragement. He knew how to put heart into people who had lost hope. He had skill to fling a sunrise into the life that had grown dark and black with night. Despair fled at the sound of his footstep, and despondency simply could not endure the sight of him. He was a good man, and, being good, he was generous in his judgments, generous in the use of his substance. He was so good that he won a new name, the Son of Consolation. In fact, he was so good that we cannot fail to see a family resemblance between him and Jesus Christ, whose goodness was goodness in perfection.

Blessed, therefore, is the man who really longs to be good. He is longing for the best. This is true because he is in quest of something that he can never know apart from God. To hunger and thirst after righteousness is, therefore, to hunger and thirst after Jesus Christ himself. Blessed is the man who has a conscious hunger after God. Blessed is he who not only possesses this hunger in regard to himself, but in regard to others as well. Blessed is the man who yearns with passionate longing that he himself and all men come into possession of vital goodness. Blessed is he who longs that he himself and the whole world shall become Christlike.

And, mark you, this longing is intense. Hunger is not a lukewarm something. It soon becomes a gnawing pain. It soon becomes an agony so intense that a crust of bread would be of more value than any jewel that glitters on the finger of wealth. Thirst is more painful still. A soldier, returned from the front, said that he lay for long hours in the trenches without water. "I became thirsty," he declared. "I became so thirsty that I would gladly have given my right arm for one drink of water. I became so thirsty that I would have given both my arms for one drink of water. I became so thirsty that I would have given my life for one drink of water." Jacob was thirsty when he cried desperately: "I will not let thee go, except thou bless me." John Knox was thirsty when he cried: "Give me Scotland, or I die." And Jesus Christ says: "Blessed are they that hunger and thirst after righteousness, that long intensely for goodness; for they shall be filled."

IV

Why are such blessed?

1. They are blessed in that such hungering and thirsting denotes that they are already in some measure the possessors of that for which they hunger and thirst. To really yearn to be good and to have others so is impossible for one who is not in some measure good already. God takes the will for the deed. When David longed to build the temple he was forbidden. But the temple was really his, after all. God said: "Whereas it was in thine heart to build me an house unto my name, thou didst well that it was in thine heart." "It is not what man does," said Browning, "but what man would do that exalts him." Certainly there is real exaltation in this hungering and thirsting after righteousness.

2. Such hungering and thirsting lead with absolute certainty to a fuller possession and a richer, more abiding satisfaction. They lead also to larger

usefulness. The one that so hungers and thirsts will seek and, seeking, will find. He will come to know from actual experience the truth of what Jesus said when he cried: "He that cometh to me shall never hunger, and he that believeth on me shall never thirst." He shall also experience the truth of that other great word: "If any man thirst, let him come to me and drink. . . . He that believeth on me as the Scripture hath said, out of his inner life shall flow rivers of living water." That is, he will find satisfaction for himself and be a means of bringing satisfaction to others.

This does not mean, of course, that when we have come to Jesus he meets our needs once and for all, so that we never need come any more. It rather means that we shall ever go on hungering and thirsting as those do who are in normal health, but that for every hunger and every thirst there shall be abiding satisfaction. It means that we shall consistently be saying with the governor of the feast: "Thou hast kept the good wine until now." This we shall say the first time we kiss the brimming draft. This we shall say as we get deeper into the years and deeper into the knowledge of Jesus. This we shall say as we come to the end of the journey, as we push our weary feet into the shadows. This we shall say when we wake in his likeness on the other side. Surely, "Blessed are they which do hunger and thirst after righteousness: for they shall be satisfied." They shall be satisfied in the here and now and satisfied in the eternal yonder.

V

THE MERCIFUL

Matthew 5: 7

"Blessed are the merciful: for they shall obtain mercy."

SPEAKING out of my own experience, I find this the most arresting of all the beatitudes. There is not one of them that, taken to heart, does not bring conviction. There is not one that does not tend to drive us to our knees in pentinence and prayer. But this, I think, is the most searching. It brings to mind our hasty judgments, our sharp criticisms, our callousness in the presence of heartache and pain. As we listen to it we feel that this prayer is the most fitting that we can pray: "God be merciful unto me a sinner."

I

Now, to be merciful is far more than to be possessed of a facility for shedding tears. Of course the merciful sometimes weep In the presence of the grief of Martha and Mary over the death of their brother, Jesus could not restrain his tears. In another place we read that he beheld the city and wept over it. There must have been something tremendously startling about the weeping of this strong and sunny man. Doubtless those who saw his face wet with tears were profoundly impressed. And how meaningful were his tears! They were born of emotions that were tremendously dynamic. But those emotions did not exhaust themselves in a mere flood of tears. "Jesus wept." But he did far more than weep: he gave himself even unto death to serving and saving of those over whom he wept.

But there are those who weep easily and copiously, whose tears are without any meaning or worth. There is no driving power in them. They only bring an added weakness. I am told that there was once a steamboat that after every whistle had to stop and get up steam again. Its driving power exhausted itself in one trumpet blast. There is often a like result from weeping of certain emotional folks. Through their tears all the driving power of their emotions escapes. Such often feel themselves very pious and very merciful because of their facility for weeping. But their tears are vain and futile because they lead to no helpful crusade. In fact, they lead to no activity at all except the use of a pocket handkerchief or the application of a powder puff.

To be merciful is to do something more than give and serve. Mercifulness is more than passing out sandwiches and hot coffee to down-and-outs. It is more than subscribing to the Community Fund or driving an ambulance. Not that a merciful man will not do all these when necessity requires. He will do them gladly. But it is possible to do them all and yet not be merciful. Rome fed and amused her

THE MERCIFUL

populace to their undoing. But she did not for that reason show herself merciful. When Sir Launfal set out on his search for the Holy Grail, he saw a repulsive beggar crouched by his gate who asked him for alms. The knight did not refuse, nor did he give him a cheap and worthless gift. He gave him real gold. But he gave it with loathing and totally without any mercy in his heart. Therefore, hungry though the beggar was, he could not accept this loveless gift.

> "The beggar left the coin in the dust;
> Better to me the poor man's crust,
> Though he turn me empty from his door."

Thackeray, in his lecture on Swift, gives us a picture of the Dean's activities in the interest of others. He gave himself rather freely to the service of his fellows, but he was not a merciful man. Thackeray says that he insulted while he served, and that, therefore, he would rather have had a potato and a kind word from Goldsmith than to have been beholden to the great Dean for a guinea and a dinner.

What, then, is to be merciful? Mercifulness is primarily a thing of the inner life. It is a disposition of the soul. It is to be possessed of a forgiving spirit. It is to have a heart of pity and compassion. It is to have Christ's way of looking at men. It is to feel toward our friends and our foes somewhat as Christ felt toward his. It is to have Christ's attitude toward the sinful and the suffering. It is to feel somewhat as he felt toward those who were outcasts and toward those who had gone hopelessly wrong. It is to have a heart made warm with the springtime of genuine brotherliness.

II

Now, of course, if this springtime of brotherliness is in the heart, it will give an account of itself in outward conduct. Even if springtime comes to this wintry and seemingly dead world of ours it cannot keep the fact a secret. It will tell the story of its coming in a thousand voices. It will tell it through the bursting buds of the trees. It will tell it in the song of the catbird among the apple blossoms. It will tell it in the blush of the rose. Even the listless dirt beneath our feet will proclaim it.

> "Every clod feels the stir of might,
>   An instinct within it that reaches and towers,
> And groping blindly above it for light,
>   Climbs to a soul and the grass and the flowers."

Even so, if the springtime of mercy is in our hearts it will make itself known in a multitude of ways. We mention only a very few of these.

1. If we are merciful, we are going to be kindly in our judgments. We are going to search for the best in our fellows instead of for the worst. We are going to seek extenuating circumstances rather than those that incriminate and prove guilt. We are going to be slow to condemn and quick to commend. And this we shall do not simply from a sense of duty. Mercy is not merely a thing of duty.

> "The quality of mercy is not strained;
> It droppeth as the gentle rain from heaven
> Upon the place beneath."

THE MERCIFUL

It is spontaneous expression of a loving heart. If we are merciful, we shall naturally think and say the best possible of our erring brother.

> "When on the fair fame of friend or foe
>   The shadow of disgrace shall fall, instead
> Of words of blame, or proof of thus and so,
>   Let something good be said.
>
> Forget not that no fellow being yet
>   May fall so low but love may lift his head:
> Even the cheek of shame with tears is wet,
>   If something good be said.
>
> And so I charge you, by the thorny crown,
>   And by the cross on which the Saviour bled,
> And by your own soul's hope of fair renown,
>   Let something good be said."

2. The merciful man gives and serves. "A certain man went down from Jerusalem to Jericho, and fell among thieves, which stripped him of his raiment, and wounded him, and departed, leaving him half dead. And by chance there came down a certain priest that way: and when he saw him, he passed by on the other side. And likewise a Levite, when he was at the place, came and looked on him, and passed by on the other side. But a certain Samaritan, as he journeyed, came where he was: and when he saw him, he had compassion on him. And went to him, and bound up his wounds, pouring in oil and wine, and set him on his own beast, and brought him to an inn, and took care of him." And the world has remembered this nameless Samaritan through all the centuries. It will remember him to the end of time.

This it will do, not because he was rich, not because he was a genius, not because he was a great physician, but solely because he was merciful. And, being merciful, he could not withhold his services from one who was in need.

The priest and Levite, on the other hand, share with each other an immortality of shame. This is the case not because they assisted in the robbery. They did not steal the few shreds of clothing that the brigands might have left him. They did not inflict other wounds in addition to those from which the half-dead man was already suffering. They only passed by without doing anything. Thus they showed themselves to be without mercy. Had the officers of the city of Jerusalem set out to arrest those responsible for this crime, they would have confined their search to the fastnesses of the mountains. They would have looked only for certain red-handed highwaymen. They would have never thought of disturbing the complacent priest and the self-satisfied Levite. But Christ dares to set these two in the prisoners' dock along with the robbers. They were all alike in this, that they were lacking in mercy.

Of course the merciful man does not confine his ministry to the giving of his material substance. There are times when our fellows need such help and need it desperately, and when sure need arises it is certainly our duty to meet it. This kind of service we are rendering just now better than ever before. I am sure there was never a time when men gave such help so freely as to-day. But there are other needs that we must meet. There may be those in our city who are actually hungry for physical bread. But for every one of these there are thousands that are in need of the Bread of Life. There may be those who are shivering with cold from lack of adequate clothing or for want of a fire to keep them warm. But for every one of these there are thousands who are shivering in their souls for lack of sympathy or encouragement or the handclasp of a brother. The merciful man does more than say, "I am sorry"; he comes to our relief and gets under our load with us.

3. Finally, the merciful man is forgiving. He refuses to nurse a grudge. He flings hate out of his heart as a thing that is deadly and damning. He loves his enemies. He blesses those that curse him and prays for those that despitefully use and persecute him. And in so doing he shows himself big with something of the bigness of Christ.

When William E. Gladstone was Chancellor of the Exchequer he sent down to the Treasury for certain statistics upon which he was to base his budget proposals. The statistician made a mistake. But Gladstone was so sure of this man's accuracy that he did not take time to verify his figures. He went before the House of Commons and made his speech, basing his appeal on the incorrect figures that had been given him. His speech was no sooner published than the newspapers exposed its glaring inaccuracies. Gladstone was naturally overwhelmed with embarrassment. He went to his office and sent at once for the statistician who was responsible for his humiliating situation. The man came, full of fear and shame, certain that he was going to lose his position. But, instead, Mr. Gladstone said: "I know how much you must be disturbed over what has happened, and I have sent for you to put you at your ease. For a long time you have been engaged in handling the intricacies of the national accounts, and this is the first mistake that you have made. I want to congratulate you and express to you my keen appreciation." It took a big man to do that, big with the bigness of the truly merciful.

III

Now, if we are eager to become merciful we might begin by remembering our own need of mercy. "Brethren, if a man be overtaken in a fault, ye which are spiritual restore such an one in the spirit of meekness, considering thyself." If we do seriously consider ourselves, we are likely to realize that the faults that we most sharply condemn in others are often those of which we ourselves are guilty. If we are at all acquainted with our own sinful hearts, we cannot but realize that it is only of the amazing mercy of God that we are any better than the chief of sinners. Therefore, since we have so much for which we must be forgiven, we ought to be ready to forgive. That was a wise and just word that John Wesley spoke to Governor Oglethorpe. The Governor was berating a servant who had just

THE MERCIFUL

drunk all his favorite wine. "I will be avenged," he cried. "I never forgive." "In that case," said Mr. Wesley, "I hope you never sin." It is a fitting word for every one of us.

Then, we need to consider how imperfectly we often know those whom we condemn. If we knew all, we might find it easier to forgive all. There is a story of a certain preacher who was one day having his shoes shined. He was in a bit of a hurry. When he thought it was about time for the task to be finished, he looked down only to find his shoes in worse condition than they were at the beginning. He spoke sharply to the little bootblack. It was then that the little fellow looked up and showed a face that was wet with tears. "I am sorry, sir," he said. "But my mother died this morning, and I am trying to make a little money to buy some flowers to put on her coffin." And the preacher saw that it was his tears falling on his shoes that was making it impossible for him to shine them. Of course all condemnation died in his heart. "Since that experience," he declared, "I have gone about my ministry with a new outlook. I feel now as if I were walking over a battle field after the battle, caring for the wounded and the dying."

But there is no being merciful in the deepest sense without the help of Christ. "He delighteth in mercy." If we come to share his nature, if he walks with us, if he dwells within us through the Holy Spirit, then we shall share in his tenderheartedness and his willingness to forgive. We shall look upon needy men everywhere with eyes full of pity and compassion. True mercifulness is a gift. Apart from Jesus Christ we can never attain it. But he makes it possible even for the most callous and self-centered.

IV

The blessing promised to the merciful is that they shall obtain mercy. This does not mean, of course, that our Lord is hiring us to be merciful. It does not mean that if we show an ounce of mercy that same amount shall be exactly weighed out to us. Christ is not a merchant who sells; he is a Saviour who gives. The merciful receive mercy because they are capable of receiving it. To be wanting in mercy is to make the receiving of mercy an impossibility.

That the merciful obtain mercy is true in some measure in our everyday relationships. The attitude of men toward ourselves depends largely upon our attitude toward them. If folks are not friendly with you, the chances are that it is because you are not friendly with them. If nobody ever does you a kindness, it is exceedingly likely that you yourself never do a kindness. If the back of every man's hand is toward you, that is pretty good evidence that the back of your hand is toward every man. This I say, not forgetting that the most merciful Man that ever lived was hung on a cross.

Then the merciful always and everywhere obtain mercy from God, while the unforgiving make the receiving of mercy impossible. How strikingly Jesus

THE MERCIFUL

emphasizes this truth in his story of that unforgiving debtor. He owed an enormous sum. It was in the millions. When he could not pay, his creditor ordered that he be cast into prison and that his wife and children be sold into slavery, so that as much as possible might be realized. But the debtor's heart was broken and he flung himself in an abandon of grief at the feet of his lord and said: "Have patience with me, and I will pay thee all." Of course he could never have paid, but the creditor's heart was touched. He was a merciful man. He then and there forgave him all the debt.

But that forgiven man went out and met one of his fellows who owed him a sum that was a mere trifle. When he demanded payment, his debtor fell at his feet and prayed the same prayer that had been on his own lips a short while before. But he flatly refused to hear. Instead he had the man thrown into prison. And what was the outcome? This unforgiving creditor had his pardon canceled, and he himself was arrested and cast into prison. "So likewise," Jesus concludes, "shall my Heavenly Father do also unto you, if ye from your hearts forgive not every one his brother their trespasses." God can no more forgive the unforgiving than he can make twice two eight. This is true because when God forgives he creates within us a new heart of love. But a new heart of love is impossible so long as we cling to the old heart of hate. Therefore to refuse to show mercy is to shut the door of mercy in our own faces.

72 THE SERMON ON THE MOUNT

But whenever we show mercy or even a real willingness to be merciful, then we surely obtain mercy.

In one of my pastorates there was a mother whose daughter went wrong. That mother was an upright woman, but she was as cold as ice and hard as a nail. When she heard the wretched news, instead of going to her wayward daughter and putting her arms around her and trying to help her, she vowed that never again would she allow that unfortunate daughter to cross the threshold of her home and never again would she look into her face. And the tragedy of it was that she meant it. So the girl was sent away to a rescue home in the city.

But as her time drew near, the poor thing became desperately heartsick and homesick. She ran away from the rescue home and came to knock on the door of her mother's home, but it was shut in her face. Then she went across the field to where one of her father's tenants lived, and there in the most delicate and trying moment that ever comes to a woman's soul she was in large measure alone. When the little laddie was three weeks of age a friend came to me with this question: "Did you know that the folks that took Mary in are going to turn her out?" "No," I answered. "But has she any other place to go?" "No," was the reply. "Will not her mother take her back?" I continued. Again my friend answered in the negative. "You see," he said, "her mother has forbidden Mary's name to be mentioned in her presence. Besides, she has heart failure, and everybody believes that if her name should be

THE MERCIFUL

mentioned it would throw her into such a rage that it would be the death of her."

With this information I went to my study. After a season of prayer I rose from my knees to go to see this woman, highly resolved to kill her, provided that should be the result of my speaking to her about her daughter. I found her unbelievably bitter. She went deadly white as I told her why I had come. And as I spoke to her, using great plainness of speech, she burst into tears, partly, I think, from grief and fear and partly from anger. Then I made my final plea. I asked her to let me go for her daughter. I told her that I would be glad to go and bring her home. But she only answered: "I can't let you." At last she said: "But I will do this, I will ask God to help me." With that I went away, fearing that I had accomplished nothing.

That evening another friend met me on the street and said: "Did you know that Mary had gone home?" "No," I said, "but I am going to see." I hurried to the parsonage. Our houses stood back to back. I ran through my back yard and garden and through the garden and back yard of this mother. As I stood there in the rain, I heard the rocking of a straight-back chair and the cracked voice of a grandmother singing a lullaby. The last service I performed before leaving the little village, as I did in a few days, was to go at the invitation of this grandmother and baptize the little fellow that had come into the world branded by shame in the eyes of society, but with the sanctifying kiss of his

Heavenly Father upon his lips and with a right to a chance. And the most wonderful part of it all was the change that had taken place in the face of that grandmother. The hardness and coldness and frozen hate had passed away, and the peace of heaven looked out from her kindly eyes. She had become merciful, and in so doing she had obtained mercy.

VI

THE VISION SPLENDID

Matthew 5: 8

"Blessed are the pure in heart: for they shall see God."

I

This is the most familiar of the beatitudes and the best loved. It is not difficult to see why this is the case. It speaks of the promise and possibility of our seeing God.

1. This possibility is a badge of our greatness. It lifts us to immeasurable heights above all other creatures of the earth. There are those who are very fond of telling us how close akin the embryonic man is to the embryonic monkey. They are so nearly alike that one cannot tell them apart. Yet they are traveling roadways that separate them by distances infinitely wider apart than the spaces between the stars. The one is traveling toward a life that is, in the very nature of things, of the earth earthy. The other is headed toward amazing possibilities. He is traveling toward a capacity for a clear vision of God. That is the pledge of his vast superiority. Surely the Psalmist was right in the light of this fact when he said: "Thou hast made him a little lower than God, and hast crowned him with glory and honor."

2. Not only does this beatitude tell of man's highest possibilities, it also tells of his deepest longings. The desire to see God is characteristic of the race. When Philip said, "Lord, show us the Father, and it is enough," he was voicing a longing that was uttered long before Abraham left Ur of the Chaldees to journey into the unknown. It was uttered long before the towers of Babylon ever lifted their tall heads to gaze down upon the smiling waters of the Euphrates. It is a cry that is older than civilization. It is older than human history. It is as old as man. Throughout all the centuries man has cried either articulately or inarticulately: "O that I knew where I might find Him! that I might come even to his seat!"

3. Then, this beatitude not only speaks home to our deepest longings, but also to our supreme need. As I am speaking to you, I cannot but be conscious of the fact that you have come together at this hour with many different burdens and with many pressing needs. Some have come from beside graves so distressingly new. Some have come from separations more tragic than the separations caused by death. Some of you are the slaves of habits from which you cannot break away. You have resolved and re-resolved only to become worse entangled. You have cursed yourself for a fool only to have the shackles tightened about your wrists. Some are spending life for a poor second best, getting very little when you might get so much. What is the one big need of every one of us? It is just this: a clear

THE VISION SPLENDID

and satisfying vision of God. Those of you who are seeing him who is invisible know that your deepest needs have been met. You know that every iron gate opens of its own accord as you approach it in his fellowship. No wonder, therefore, that we love this beatitude. It is a pledge of our greatness. It offers the satisfaction of our most intense hungers and of our deepest needs.

II

What is it to see God? Of course to see God is not to look upon him with our natural eye. The truth is that the one who sees only what meets the eye sees very little. There was a poet once who declared that he could see in the meanest flower that blows thoughts that lay too deep for tears. That is what made him a poet. There were multitudes that looked upon Jesus and saw nothing of winsomeness in him. To them he was as a root out of dry ground, utterly without form or comeliness. They looked upon him and trudged on their weary and monotonous ways as totally unhelped as if they had looked upon the face of a mummy.

But there were others who saw him with different eyes. As they looked into his face they became conscious of God. As they fellowshiped with him they said: "Thou art the Christ, the Son of the living God." And when he had gone home to heaven they still saw him. They still realized him as one "closer than breathing, and nearer than hands and feet." Paul, who had never looked on his face in the flesh, said: "Have I not seen Jesus Christ our Lord? . . . I know whom I have believed, and am persuaded that he is able to keep that which I have committed unto him against that day."

To see God, then, is to realize him, to be sure of him. It is to have life made radiant by the most blessed of all certainties, the certainty of God. And, mark you, this is an experience that takes place in the here and now. So often we read this beatitude and postpone its rich promise to some far-off to-morrow. "Blessed are the pure in heart, for they shall see God," when they wake in his likeness on the other side. That is true, certainly; but the pure in heart do not have to wait until then. They see him in the here and now. They enter into his fellowship in the life that now is. The truth is that if we do not see him in the here and now we have no promise of seeing him at all. If we do not get acquainted with him in this present to-day, we have no slightest guarantee of enjoying his fellowship in that distant to-morrow. To see God, therefore, is to be sure of him, to realize him amidst all the laughter and tears of the life that now is.

III

What are some of the blessings that come as a result of this vision splendid?

1. To see God is to see one's self. Job was a character of unusual worth and beauty. He was tragically afflicted in his body. One fancies, at times, that he was even more afflicted through his

friends. They came to tell him, as pain tortured him, that the whole tragedy was the result of his sin. Job denied it with hot indignation, and we cannot help siding with him. We applaud him as he maintains his integrity. But by and by a vision of God bursts upon him. Then all Job's self-sufficiency is gone, his knees go weak, and in deep humility he cries: "I have heard of thee by the hearing of the ear: but now mine eye seeth thee: wherefore I abhor myself, and repent in dust and ashes."

Here is another man, certainly one of the cleanest and most upright of his day. He is telling us of the personal experience that made him the man that he became. "In the year that King Uzziah died, I saw the Lord." And what was the outcome of the vision? In the brightness of that light he also saw himself. And what he saw caused him to put his lips to the dust and cry: "I am a man of unclean lips, and I dwell in the midst of a people of unclean lips." Similar was the effect upon the repentant robber. His companion in crime could see the visible Christ as well as himself. But seeing only that, he joined with the mob in their howls of abuse. But this greater robber saw more deeply. He penetrated the disguise of weakness. He penetrated the dusky disguise of death itself and saw the real Christ, and that vision smote him with a conviction of his own deep guilt. "Dost thou not fear God, seeing thou art in the same condemnation? And we indeed justly; for we receive the due reward of our deeds; but this man hath done nothing amiss."

His vision of Christ brought him, as it always does, a vision of self.

2. To see God is to be transformed. For when we see him we are always convicted of sin. Whenever there is a sense of God, there is always a sense of sin. And the opposite is also true, absolutely and always. Whenever there is no sense of sin, there is no sense of God. We are told that certain Africans never realized that they were black till they looked on the white face of David Livingstone. Then they could not help but realize it. And whenever we see ourselves in the light of the divine countenance, we never fail to come to a realization of our guilt. To see God is always to cry with the prophet: "Unclean, unclean!"

But the vision does more for us than simply show us our own sinfulness. It also brings us cleansing from sin. Was it not so in the case of Isaiah? No sooner had he confessed his sin than he became conscious of cleansing by the power of God. Was it not so in the case of the dying robber? Having confessed his own guilt, he dares to pray the most amazing prayer ever uttered, I think: "Lord, remember me when thou comest into thy kingdom." "I know this is not the end," he seems to say. "When you have passed through this black tunnel of death, when you have come out under the clear skies of your kingdom, don't forget the needy, sin-stained robber at whose side you died." And Jesus gave an answer that made the robber forgetful of the pangs of the cross: "To-day thou shalt be with me in paradise."

How strikingly the transforming power of God is illustrated in the life of Jacob! In his earlier years Jacob is exceedingly disappointing. You could not love him if you wanted to. He is a creature of shifts and trickery. He delights to live by his wits. Laban is no paragon of honesty himself, but he is no match for his wily nephew. Jacob knows all the tricks of the trade. Had he been in the dry goods business instead of handling live stock, I am confident that he would have had no less than a half dozen successful fires during his sojourn with Uncle Laban. As it is, he disappears over the plains one day driving the better part of what had been his uncle's herds before him. He has been successful. He has succeeded in a most dangerous fashion, by trickery. He is going now to possess his inheritance with a feeling that he has made sin to pay. But in that awful night by the ford something happens to him. From a spiritual pauper he becomes a prince. As he limped away next morning, the sun that looked over the eastern hills was not so bright as the light that shone in his heart. And when they asked him how the marvelous change had been wrought, he answered: "I have seen God face to face."

3. To see God is to come into possession of a new and steadfast courage. That is a bracing word that the writer to the Hebrews uses in his story of Moses. "He endured," he tells us. There was much opposition from the authorities of Egypt, but he en-

dured. There was much opposition among his own people, but he endured. His hopes were long deferred, but he endured. There was persistent whining, there was a distressing lack of patience, but he endured. They threw mud at him instead of flowers, but he endured. How steadfast he was, how courageous, how dauntless! What is the secret of it all? "He endured as seeing Him who is invisible." There is a courage, a steadfastness, a gallant staunchness that belong to those that see God that cannot be won except through such high vision.

4. Then, to see God is to become in the highest sense useful. This is true, in the first place, because it is the man who has seen God who is the most eager to serve. To see him is to be gripped with a holy passion to share your vision with others. How strikingly this is illustrated throughout the Scriptures and throughout the history of the Church! No sooner does God call for volunteers than Isaiah replies eagerly: "Here am I; send me." How bent on giving were those who had been with the Lord Jesus! The world did not think that it wanted their story. It paid them with ostracism, with stones and dungeons and wild beasts and forests of crosses. But it could not destroy their passion for giving. They continued to declare by word and deed: "We cannot but speak the things that we have seen and heard."

Then, it is the man who has seen God who is the most capable of giving. There is absolutely no service that one human being can render another that is quite so high and helpful as the giving of a sense of God. Our first conviction of the reality of God often comes to us through some friend or loved one. Listen to Ruth, for instance, as she makes about the most beautiful confession of love and faith ever uttered: "Entreat me not to leave thee, or to return from following after thee: for whither thou goest, I will go; and where thou lodgest, I will lodge; thy people shall by my people, and thy God my God: . . . the Lord do so to me, and more also, if aught but death part thee and me." How did Ruth come to turn her back on the gods of her people and give herself to the God of Israel? It was through the vision of God that she had had in the life of Naomi. As she looked into that sweet face, as she read that tender heart, she said: "If God is like you, then he shall have me and mine forever."

To be able to give a sense of God, I repeat, is the highest of all services. Blessed are the children that are able to see in the beautiful and radiant lives of their parents something that can only be accounted for in terms of God. Blessed are those who by the sweet and heavenly atmosphere of the home are made to feel "surely God is in this place." Blessed the Sunday school teacher that can bring to the class Sunday by Sunday a sense of God. Such a teacher may be very limited in knowledge, very limited in a thousand ways; but in spite of all limitations, such an one will leave a blessing behind that none but God can fully estimate. Blessed is the preacher that can so speak as to make his hearers look past him into that Face that is "altogether lovely and the fairest of ten thousand." God pity him if those that hear him sympathetically must say, as a very cultured and hungry-hearted gentleman said recently of a certain minister that he had heard: "He interested me, instructed me, even fascinated me, but he left me with no sense of God." Surely, of all people that enrich us, of all those to whom we owe unpayable debts, there is none to whom we are quite so indebted as to him who brings to us a sense of God. And the only man who can do this is the man who has himself seen God.

IV

Now, how shall we see God? What roadway can we take with the assurance of the coming into possession of this vision splendid?

Let us begin with the sure conviction that to see God is a possibility that is within reach of every one of us. It is not simply for some aged saint who is nearing the sunset and evening star. It is not simply for the minister. It is not simply for some choice soul here and there. Here is a prize of supreme worth that is within reach of every heart that is willing to lay hold of it. Let us grip that truth and refuse to let it go. Say to your own needy heart: "This blessing is for me. It is my privilege to see God, to realize him. It is my privilege to live in the realm of radiant certainty."

Having become convinced that the blessing is for yourself, the next step is to meet the conditions.

"Blessed are the pure in heart: for they shall see God." What is it to be pure in heart? On the surface it sounds forbidding. It suggests the impossible. But to be pure in heart does not mean sinlessness. Jesus is not saying: "Blessed are the perfect: for they shall see God." To be pure in heart is to be simple, sincere, whole-hearted. Jesus was uttering the same truth in different words when he said: "If any man is willing to do his will, he shall know of the doctrine." Blessed is the fully surrendered man, for he shall know, he shall see God.

This is the clear teaching of the New Testament. It is also the teaching of experience. Its truth has been demonstrated in countless millions of lives. E. Stanley Jones tells us that while he was visiting Gandhi a Sadhu came eight hundred miles to ask Gandhi two questions. The questions were these: "How can I get rid of sin, and how can I find God?" Having asked Gandhi, the seeker after God came to ask Jones the same questions. He said to the inquirer: "Before I answer you, would you mind telling me what Gandhi told you?" "No, I don't mind telling you," he answered. "He told me to sit down in one place and not roam about as the Sadhus do, but stay in one place till I had conquered my senses and my passions and worn them out, then I might find release." "Was there no offer of immediate relief?" Jones asked. "O, no," was the reply. "He said it would take a long, long time." And then he turned to Jones and said: "Now what do you say?" And this radiant missionary told him what had happened to himself. He said: "My yearning was exactly your yearning. I needed to know how to get rid of sin, and I needed to know God. But I did not need to stay in one place till I had worn out my passions; I simply turned over a bankrupt soul to Jesus Christ, and, lo, as I gave my all he gave me his all. It did not take ages, it took surrender. It did not take time, it took me."

That is a clear path that all human feet can travel. And, regardless of the starting point, he who travels it finds God. In England years ago there was a man, a pessimist and a cynic, who had become bankrupt in faith and joy and hope. One desperate night he wrote on a piece of paper something like this: "If there is a Being above who takes thought of the needs of man, if that Being will reveal his will to me, it will be my highest joy to do that will wherever it may take me and whatever it may involve." And what was the outcome? That man spent forty years in the enervating climate of India as a medical missionary without ever a vacation. He was willing to do His will, therefore he came to know. He was pure in heart, therefore he saw God. The same may happen to every man, for this is forever true: "Blessed are the pure in heart; for they shall see God."

VII

THE PEACEMAKERS

Matthew 5: 9

"Blessed are the peacemakers: for they shall be called the children of God."

"Blessed are the peacemakers." For nineteen centuries this great word has been knocking at the shut doors of men's hearts, largely in vain. We have said "Yes" with our lips, but by our lives we have said: "Blessed are the sowers of discord. Blessed are the fomenters of strife. Blessed are the war makers." But Christ in loving patience still proclaims that it is the peacemakers who are blessed.

I

Now, to make peace is to do far more than merely abolish strife. To make peace is to do more than cause men or nations to be peaceable. We may keep the peace without having peace. We may bring about a cessation of strife without in any real sense being peacemakers. The Roman Empire brought about peace within her borders, but she was not a peacemaker according to the meaning of Jesus. Her subjects had not lost the will to fight. They kept peace through fear. They were not at war solely because the dread of Rome forced them to swallow their hate and to submit with sullen rage to their fortune.

When I was a boy we owned two magnificent dogs. These dogs were of different breed. They had a natural antipathy to each other. Now and then, they would come to open war. When they did so they fought to utter exhaustion. Having reached this state, they would cease to tear at each other, but they would still glare at each other in such a fashion as to indicate that the only reason they were not fighting was because they could not. And that was the impression that one received as he traveled among the nations of Europe just after the World War. One could not but feel that the only reason they were not at each other's throats was because they had already fought to complete exhaustion. They had been bled white. Therefore the peace that existed was a peace born, not of good will, but of weakness. It was a purely negative peace.

Then, there may be peace that is the outcome of mere indifference. Rip Van Winkle and his wife were accustomed to have some very stormy sessions in their humble little home. But by and by these domestic wars ceased. The noise of conflict was no longer heard. How had this peace come about? It had not come because husband and wife had arrived at a better understanding. It had not come because they had agreed, out of mutual love, to be more forbearing. There was peace because one day Rip took his musket upon his shoulder and strolled off

THE PEACEMAKERS

into the mountains for a twenty-year nap. I read some months ago where two deadly enemies met and shot each other to death. As they lay side by side they were at peace, but it was the peace of indifference, it was the peace of death. Therefore it was a purely negative something.

But the peacemaker of whom Jesus speaks does a positive work. He puts an end to strife by the bringing in of its opposite. He does not pull up the noxious weeds of discord and enmity and hate one by one and leave the garden bare. He rather sows and cultivates such a luxuriant crop of the flowers of the Spirit—love, joy, peace, long-suffering—that the disturbing weeds are all crowded out. He drives out suspicion by confidence, enmity and misunderstanding by understanding and good will. He puts brotherliness in the place of unbrotherliness. He puts love in the place of hate. Through his ministry men not only cease to fear each other and to fight each other, but they come to love and to trust each other. He does more than take the sword and break it into fragments. He does more than blunt the spear and burn its shaft. He beats the sword into a plowshare, and the spear into a pruning hook. He converts the implements of war and waste into implements of peace and prosperity. He overcomes evil with good.

II

Now, that peacemakers are needed in our world no one will deny. The peacemaker is a benefactor. I take it that he is the supreme benefactor.

1. We need peacemakers because there is such a widespread lack of peace. Strife and discord, hate and misunderstanding are on every hand. This I say not minimizing the marvelous advancements that have been made. No man can look upon our world with open eyes and fail to recognize that there has been encouraging progress. The fact that the Prime Minister of England has recently crossed the Atlantic to talk with our President in the interest of world peace is surely the prophecy of a better day. But there still remains much land to be possessed. In spite of all that has been done, our peace is not yet like a river. We are still far from a "parliament of man and a federation of the world."

Think, first, of the strife between man and his Maker. This strife is as old as human history. In the Eden story, man after his sin no sooner heard the voice of God walking in the garden than he hid himself. He had come to fear the One that he should have loved best. Instead of seeking God, instead of crying in his need, "O my God, where art Thou?" God had to do the seeking and cry, "Adam, where art thou?" This is an old story, I know. You may no longer believe it. But surely you believe the more modern story of your own life. Account for it how you may, some of you are keenly conscious of the fact that there is a quarrel between you and God. There are many, thank God, for whom this quarrel has been healed. But there are vast multitudes for whom it has not been healed. The supreme tragedy of their hour is that there are so many in our world that are not on friendly terms with God.

With the loss of peace between man and God there comes also the loss of peace between man and his better self. That has always been the case. To be at war with God is to have civil war within your own soul. "There is no peace, saith my God, to the wicked." If I could take my soul into my own two hands and utterly erase the image of God from it, I might have a certain kind of peace apart from God. But this I cannot do. It has been well said that no man can be as bad as he wants to be. The hogs may be content within the pigsty of the far country. But for the prodigal, contentment is impossible. He was made for something better. He is persistently tormented by memories of his father. He is made miserable and restless by dreams of his finer possibilities.

"My soul cleaveth unto the dust" is the cry of the Psalmist. Then why does he not lay hold on the dust and be content? Because he cannot. The cleaving is all very real, but that is only half the story. "My soul cleaveth unto the dust; quicken thou me according to thy word." That is the other half. While he cleaves to the dust, he also aspires to the heights. While with one hand he fingers the mud, with the other he reaches after the stars. Why does not the sea lie down within its far-flung shores and be at rest? Because the heights will not let it alone. When it is minded to become content with the earth, the voices of cloudland call it.

Therefore it is always tossing and restless. And man is forever like that troubled sea till he finds rest in God.

Then there is widespread discord and strife between man and man. Men glare at each other individually. Group looks askance at group. Racial prejudices and racial hates abound. Nation glares at nation, and each proclaims itself *the people*. Many Americans still say, "America first"; Many British, "England first;" Germans, "Germany first." We are still far from seeing in every man a brother for whom Christ died. We are still far from a brotherhood of nations.

2. Then we need peacemakers because strife and enmity and hate are so costly. It is certainly true that the most expensive something in all the world is hate. Think of its cost to the individual. Enmity between God and man is the fountain source of all wretchedness. It was when Paul looked to the heights and went toward the depths that he cried, "O wretched man that I am!" Such hostility makes for ineffectiveness. This it does because it makes for a divided personality. "Unite my heart to fear thy name" is the wisest of prayers. It is the only way that we can come to the fullness o four powers. A divided personality means at once the loss of happiness and the loss of our highest effectiveness. A unified personality, on the other hand, means the attainment of both peace and power.

How costly is hate between man and man! I know of nothing that is so deadly as hating some-

THE PEACEMAKERS

body. What havoc it sometimes works to the one who is hated! What havoc it always works to the hater! How many an organization has been disrupted by it? How many a church has had its usefulness impaired and the thews of its spiritual strength clipped by it! When given right of way it changes our homes into hells and puts within our hearts that which bites like a serpent and stings like an adder.

How all but infinite has been the cost of hate between section and section, nation and nation! War has certainly been a supreme curse of the world. It is the most deadly foe of mankind. It kills men's bodies, and too often their souls as well. Every war brings in its wake an aftermath of blighted ideals and lowered moral standards. Think of the cost of the World War. Its cost in material wealth was incredibly great. But that was as nothing in comparison with its cost in other directions. It is estimated that its total casualties up to the present time are more than thirty millions of human lives. And so many of them were our choicest and our best.

> "Where are you going, Young Fellow, My Lad,
>   On this glittering morn of May?
>   I am going to join the colors, Dad,
>   They are wanting men, they say.
>   But you are only a boy, Young Fellow, My Lad,
>   You are not obliged to go.
>   I'm seventeen and a quarter, Dad,
>   And ever so strong, you know.

So you are off to France, Young Fellow, My Lad?
   And you are looking so fit and bright.
I'm dreadfully sorry to leave you, Dad,
   But I feel that I am doing right.
God bless you and keep you, Young Fellow, My Lad,
   For you are all my life, you know.
Don't worry, I'll soon be back, dear Dad,
   And I'm awfully proud to go.

What is the matter, Young Fellow, My Lad?
   No letter again to-day?
And why did the postman look so sad
   And sigh as he turned away?
I hear them say that we've gained new ground,
   But a terrible price we've paid.
God grant, my boy, that you are safe and sound,
   But O, I'm afraid, afraid!

They've told me the truth, Young Fellow, My Lad,
   And you'll never come home again.
O God, the dreams and the dreams I've had
   And the hopes I've nursed in vain!
For you passed in the night, Young Fellow, My Lad,
   But you proved in that terrible test,
Of the bursting shell and the battle hell,
   That my boy was one of the best."

War is always taking the best, and, taking them, it squanders their lives, so often for nothing and worse than nothing.

3. Finally, we need peacemakers because peace will never come of itself. Peace must be made. We may drift into war. We may drowse and trifle our way into confusion and conflict. But if peace is ever realized it must be through conscious, persistent, sacrificial effort. We must do more than dream of peace; we must make it. And that we can do.

Every soul may become a peacemaker. It is impossible for all of us to make fortunes. We cannot all make a great noise in the world. We cannot all make great names. But we can do something far better: we can all make peace, and in so doing invest ourselves for the attaining of the highest possible good.

III

Now, if we are to make peace, how are we to go about it? How is peace to be made? It is not going to be made through hate. That sounds obvious to the point of utter triteness, I know. But, as you turn the pages of history, you will see that it has not been at all obvious, even to the nations that are nominally Christian. Of course we have abandoned to some extent the idea that the way for one neighbor to get along with another is for each to carry a six-shooter. For me to mount a machine gun upon the front porch of the parsonage to defend myself against my neighbors would not be regarded as Christian. That, of course, everybody will recognize.

But somehow we are not so quick to recognize the fact that it is equally unchristian to depend on standing armies and battle ships to keep peace between nation and nation. We readily agree that one Christian cannot hate another, but we are by no means quick in our agreement that Christian nations cannot hate each other. How slow we are in learning that we cannot be Christian individually and pagans nationally! How slow we are in recognizing the obvious truth that we cannot be good Samaritans as individuals and highwaymen and priests and Levites as a nation! We cannot bring about peace between nation and nation by killing each other any more than we can bring it about between man and man.

This, I know, sounds so evident as to seem almost puerile, yet we cannot forget that it has not been long since many of our statesmen and some of our preachers were encouraging us in our fighting by saying that we were waging a war that was to end war. There are multitudes that were honestly convinced that such was the case. They had persuaded themselves that somehow love could be born out of hate and discord, and strife could be the mother of peace. But "do men gather grapes of thorns, or figs of thistles?" "Who can bring a clean thing out of an unclean?" That which is born of love is love, and that which is born of hate is hate. War is an evil, a deadly evil. Hate is an evil. The antidote for this evil is not more evil. Hate is never killed by hate. It is only increased by it. The only successful foe of evil is good.

> "For heathen heart that puts her trust
>   In reeking tube and iron shard;
> All valiant dust that builds on dust,
>   And guarding calls not thee to guard:
> For frantic boast and foolish word,
> Thy mercy on thy people, Lord!"

How, then, I repeat, are we to become peace-

THE PEACEMAKERS

makers? Our first step is putting ourselves into right relations with Jesus Christ. He is the supreme Peacemaker. He is the Prince of Peace. He came to teach us to say, "Our Father," and in so saying to see in every man a brother. He came "to gather together into one the sons of God that are scattered abroad." His last earthly prayer was that we all might be one. He declares that his one great task in the world is the gathering together of men into a brotherhood. "He that is not for me is against me, and he that gathereth not with me scattereth abroad."

What a startling declaration! Jesus here divides men into two groups. There are those who are for him and those who are against him. There are these two classes and these two only. "Some men," he declares, "enter my service. They make my plans and purposes their plans and purposes. My work becomes their work. They are with me. They struggle to make my dreams into realities. But there are others who oppose me. There are others who fight against me, who antagonize me, who add to the weight of my cross. There are those who by their opposition postpone the coming of that good day when the kingdoms of the world shall become the kingdom of the Lord and his Christ."

In this word also Jesus states with bold emphasis what is the acid test of our loyalty to himself. He declares that all those who make for strife and for discord are arrayed against him. Whoever cherishes hate in his heart, whoever makes it easier for men and women to suspect each other, to mistrust each other, that man, regardless of what his profession may be, is fighting against Christ. Whoever is hard to live with in the home, whoever is a promoter of strife between man and man, whoever makes for discord and misunderstanding within the Church, whoever preaches a patriotism of selfishness, whoever fosters sectional or national or racial prejudices —that man is surely the foe of Jesus Christ. This is true regardless of his claim to loyalty or of his professed orthodoxy. Jesus is come to break down all dividing walls. He is come to abolish unbrotherliness and hate everywhere. If your life and mine are making for the opposite, then we have arrayed ourselves against him whom we claim to serve.

On the other hand, if we are peacemakers, if by what we are and by what we do we preach a gospel of reconciliation, if we make for peace in the home, peace in the social circle, peace between nation and nation and between race and race, then we are making common cause with Jesus Christ. Then we are fighting under his banner. This is true whatever our denomination or lack of it. John brought some great news to Jesus on one occasion. "Master, we saw one casting out demons in thy name." How the heart of Jesus must have leaped for joy! But John had not finished his story. "We forbade him because he followed not with us." What a calamity! "Forbid him not," said Jesus emphatically. "He that is not against us is on our part." Whoever is making for peace in the hearts of men and for peace

THE PEACEMAKERS

in the world is a friend and servant of Jesus, and to him we give the right hand of fellowship.

Now, it is through the friends of Jesus that peace is to be made. It is said that a gentleman of saintly life stood one day in a great art gallery before a picture of Jesus. As he looked into the face of him who is the fairest of ten thousand and the one altogether lovely, his heart became strangely warmed and strangely glad. "Bless him, I love him," he said softly to himself. It so happened that there was a man at his side from another nation who overheard his exclamation. "Bless him, I love him too," this man replied. Then there was another and another, till by and by a little group stood reverently about the picture. These represented different nationalities and different races, but they were brought together in the bonds of a sweet and tender brotherhood by their mutual love for Jesus Christ. And one day nation is going to say to nation: "Bless him, we love him." One day the Occident is going to say to the Orient, and the Orient to the Occident: "Bless him, we love him." Then, and not till then, will men beat their swords into plowshares, and their spears into pruning hooks, and learn war no more. Then, and not till then, will the glory of God cover the earth as the waters cover the sea.

What, then, is our first and supreme duty as individuals? If we are to become peacemakers, our first duty is to accept the peace of Christ for ourselves. "He is our peace," Paul tells us. He brings peace between God and man. He brings peace within. That is the first step toward the realization of the great dream of world-wide peace. Have you accepted his peace for yourself? "Peace I leave with you, my peace I give unto you." Let us accept it. If in faith we really receive this peace, we shall come to feel, with the poet:

> "God hath given me birth,
> To brother all the sons of earth."

We shall go forth to a ministry of reconciliation. Our appeal will be that of Paul: "Now we are ambassadors for Christ, as though God did beseech you by us; we pray you in Christ's stead, be ye reconciled to God."

VIII

THE PERSECUTED

Matthew 5: 10-12

"Blessed are they which are persecuted for righteousness' sake: for theirs is the kingdom of heaven. Blessed are ye, when men shall revile you, and persecute you, and shall say all manner of evil against you falsely, for my sake.' Rejoice, and be exceeding glad: for great is your reward in heaven: for so persecuted they the prophets which were before you."

I

This is the last of the beatitudes. Up to this time Jesus has been describing the Christlike character. In this last beatitude he tells us the reception that this genuine Christian is to meet at the hands of the world. And what he says tends to fill us with amazement. One would certainly think that a character such as Jesus has described would meet with universal acclaim; that every man's heart would be open to him. But such, says Jesus, is not the case. On the contrary, the vital Christian is sure to meet with some form of opposition or persecution.

Now, the fact that the genuine Christian provokes opposition does not mean that this opposition is to be universal. Every real Christian will make friends. Every real Christian will surely win the loyal love of at least a few. I am not forgetting that

Jesus said; "Woe unto you when all men shall speak well of you." But he did not mean by that for us to pride ourselves on being universally hated. If it is a tragedy to have all men speak well of us, I am sure that a yet greater tragedy would be for all men to speak evil of us. What Jesus is here asserting is not that a real Christian is universally unpopular; He is emphasizing the fact that vital goodness provokes opposition.

This fact is clearly and emphatically demonstrated in his own life. Jesus not only spoke these beatitudes; he lived them to the point of perfection. He was meek, he was a peacemaker, his was the tenderest heart that ever beat. No man ever gave himself so freely to the service of others. But in spite of this he did not meet with universal acclaim. There were those who loved him with passionate devotion, but there were those who hated him with hellish hatred. There was nothing too harsh and cruel for them to say about him. They called him a gluttonous man and a winebibber. They said that he was a blasphemer, that he was crazy, that he was in league with the devil. At last they crowned him with thorns and hung him on a cross. He was done to death, not for any evil that was in him, but because of his vital goodness.

Paul also lived these beatitudes in an amazingly beautiful fashion. What a peacemaker he was! How compassionate! He felt himself in debt to all men. He was willing to spend and be spent for them; though the more he loved them, the less he was loved by them. But all men did not give him welcome. All did not approve. He stirred the most strenuous opposition. He was chased from one city to another. He had intimate acquaintance with the whipping post. Again and again he was thrust into prison. There was a day when he stood among flying stones till he could stand no longer. At last he died a martyr's death. And this is the word that he shouts across the centuries to you and me: "All that will live godly in Christ Jesus shall suffer persecution."

III

Why is it that real goodness provokes opposition? That such is the case is the plain teaching both of the New Testament and of history as well. This was the case in the days of Jesus. It will be the case till the kingdom of God is fully come. Of course this opposition will be less widespread and less intense the more the will of God is done and the more fully the kingdom of God is set up in the hearts of men. We are more tolerant and less bitter now than were the people who lived in the days of Jesus. This is the case because the kingdom is coming. We are accustomed to bewail the fact, and rightly so, that the Church of to-day is so much like the world. But there is this heartening fact, that the world is becoming more and more like the Church. Therefore persecution is not so bitter now as in other days. But it is still true that real goodness provokes opposition, and will continue, in some measure, to do so, till God fully has his way with us and the kingdoms of the world shall have become the kingdom of our Lord and his Christ.

1. A genuine Christian provokes opposition because he is different. If our Christianity has not made us different, then it is spurious. A certain little Indian girl rightly described the Christians that she knew as the folks that were different. To fail as a Christian, it is not necessary to be worse than the man of the world; it is only necessary to be like him. When Samson's temptress was seeking to know the secret of his strength, he informed her that if his vow should be broken he would then become weak and be like any other man not weaker than any other man, not worse than any other man, but only like him. The Christian is different, and, being different, he arouses opposition.

This is not saying that there are not those who will approve. We love and admire the man who dares to be unique. Yet we often resent him, too. We approve those who share our prejudices, who conform to our customs, who look at things through our eyes. Society constantly seeks to rob us of our individuality. Those daring saints who insist on accepting Christ's way of life are sure to be resented. They are certain to meet those who will dismiss them with a shrug of contempt, saying: "They are so peculiar." "If ye were of the world, the world would love its own: but because ye are not of the world, but I have chosen you out of the world, therefore the world hateth you."

2. Then, the vital Christian arouses opposition because he is a constant rebuke to our selfishness and our sin. Every man who in the power of Christ lives out these beatitudes becomes an incarnate conscience. He makes the self-centered, the worthless feel uncomfortable. Some of them he wins. Others he worries and offends. Elijah, so far as we know, had not said a word to the widow about her ungodly life. But he rebuked her by being what he was. "Art thou come unto me to call my sin to remembrance?" she asked. The vital Christian rebukes the sinful both by what he is and by what he says and does. Therefore he arouses opposition.

3. Finally, the truly Christlike man stirs opposition because he interferes. In a sense, as the world would put it, he meddles with our affairs. He rebukes our prejudices. He reminds us that God is the Father of all mankind and expects all men, regardless of race or creed or color, to live as brothers. He interferes with some of our pleasures. While telling us that no pleasure is sinful except sinful pleasure, he asserts that our sinful pleasure must be put away. If Jesus were to come to our city today he would possibly escape crucifixion, but he would certainly not be universally popular. In many so-called Christian homes he would not be welcome. His presence would change the cheap and vulgar laughter that often abounds there into embarrassed silence. And while showing him over our city, there are certain sections that we should carefully avoid.

Then, the vital Christian sometimes even dares to interfere with our business. There were those long ago who counted up their losses with hot rage just after Jesus had driven them out of the temple. Paul had his clothing torn from him and was publicly whipped and cast into prison because he interfered in the business of certain slave owners in the city of Philippi. And that mob that was aroused in Ephesus would gladly have torn him limb from limb had they been able to lay their hands upon him. And why should they not do so? He was ruining their business. They were making a most decent and respectable living by selling images of Diana. But by his preaching he was threatening to reduce them to poverty. No wonder they opposed him.

It has not been many years since slavery was looked upon as an institution that was altogether consistent with the teachings of Jesus. When men arose who declared to the contrary, they aroused the most bitter and intense opposition. They were interfering with vested interests. They seemed bent on robbing their fortunate fellows of their personal property. Even more recently the vast majority of our citizens thought it perfectly right and proper for this nation to engage in the liquor business. When those came forward who said that as a nation we had no right to sell that which tends only to blight and blast and damn, they, too, aroused bitter opposition. Nor does this opposition belong to a distant past. When the liquor question was dragged into national politics recently, how the party whip was popped over our heads and how almost every newspaper and politician sought to scourge the preachers into silence! The Church has yet a disturbing and provoking word to say about the industrial situation, and in saying it she is going to provoke opposition. Christianity is bound to be a disturbing factor in a social order that is largely unchristian.

III

Now, the nature of this opposition is somewhat different to-day from what it was in the days of Jesus. Persecution then usually had its culmination in physical violence. Christians were thrown into prison. They were burned at the stake. They were fed to wild beasts. They were hung upon forests of crosses. In Christian America we no longer employ such crude methods. And yet there are still Christians that have to face forms of persecution that, while more refined, require as genuine courage as that required of the Christians of the first century.

But there were at least two modes of persecution employed nineteen hundred years ago that are still in vogue. And we are often capable of using them quite as effectively as did they of the long ago. "Blessed are ye," said Jesus, "when men shall revile you, and . . . shall say all manner of evil against you falsely, for my sake." We can still revile, or reproach. We can still call people narrow and fanatical. We can still shrug our shoulders and laugh at them as cranks. The young man and the young woman who would dare go into the so-called best society of our city, taking their ideals with them, would be put to tests almost as sharp as those met by the Christians of the long ago. There are positions in the business and industrial world that, if filled in accordance with the principles of Jesus, would require a courage almost as stanch as that possessed by the martyrs.

And there is still another weapon that the world knows how to use; that is slander. When Jesus made himself the dauntless foe of evil, those who were its friends slandered him. They tried to destroy his good name. They said all manner of evil against him falsely. And such has been the lot of the choicest sons and daughters of God through the centuries. It is not always easy to suffer slander. Some have allowed their hearts to be broken by it. But it is a form of persecution that every great servant of mankind has had to endure. This has been true from Socrates and beyond, down to Woodrow Wilson.

IV

Now, since vital goodness certainly provokes opposition, since a genuine Christian is sure to have to face persecution, what are we to do about it? Suppose as a Christian I look up into the face of my Lord and say, "Jesus, Master, I am having a hard fight, I am meeting with strenuous opposition, I am face to face with persecution," what answer does our Lord give? He does not say, "I am sorry for you." He does not say, "How I pity you!" He

THE PERSECUTED 109

rather says, "Let me congratulate you." "Rejoice and be exceeding glad: for so persecuted they the prophets which were before you." That is, persecution for righteousness' sake is not something to whine about. It is something over which to rejoice. This is true, not because persecution is good in itself; it is true because of what such persecution indicates and the ends to which it leads if rightly borne.

1. Persecution for righteousness' sake indicates that the one so persecuted is a child of the kingdom. Mark you, the Master does not say that every man who is persecuted belongs to the kingdom. He says that that is true only of those who are persecuted for righteousness' sake. There are those who are persecuted, not because they are righteous, but because they are the opposite. They are persecuted, not because they are meek, but because they are pushful and self-assertive; not because they are merciful, but because they are harsh and cruel; not because they are peacemakers, but because they are trouble makers.

For instance, I have in mind two preachers. You could never guess who they are, therefore I can speak of them with safety. One is an extreme fundamentalist, the other is an equally extreme modernist. The fundamentalist consistently assigns all those who differ from him to the bottomless pit. The modernist would do the same, only he is too scholarly to believe in any such a crude place or to indulge in such crude language. Both are rabid and contentious. Both are gluttons for martyrdom. Seeking persecution with such diligence, they both find it. But somehow it is not easy for me to believe that they enter into the blessing that is pronounced by Jesus upon those who are persecuted for righteousness' sake.

But to be persecuted for righteousness' sake, I repeat, is an indication that the one so persecuted is a child of the King. It indicates that such a one has become a menace to the kingdom of evil. The devil is far too shrewd to turn his guns upon a foe who is spineless and who carries no threat. If you will read the second and third chapters of Revelation, you will find that every Church there mentioned that was counting for anything for the kingdom was being persecuted. It is only the dead or lukewarm Churches that are being let alone. If you are persecuted, that means that you are in great company. You are fighting shoulder to shoulder with the prophets who were before you. You are being opposed because, like them, you are counting in the good fight of faith.

2. Christ congratulates the persecuted because persecution is a pathway to spiritual growth. It is not by difficulties dodged, but by difficulties met and overcome that we become strong. A lotus land is a good place to sleep, but it is a poor place to develop rugged, Christlike character. Then, opposition rightly borne makes for spiritual growth because it drives the persecuted to their Lord. "My grace is sufficient for thee." When the situation is

especially hard, when the opposition is too great for our petty strength, then we may expect great grace, for there is always enough. John G. Paton tells of the bitter opposition that he met in the far-off Hebrides. During a season of persecution he spent one night in a tree. He could hear the savages beating the bushes beneath him, carefully searching for him in an effort to take his life. But he declared that he would gladly pass through another such experience of peril to be privileged to enjoy the assuring and comforting presence of Jesus as he did on that night.

This is one reason that the Church has always experienced its greatest power in times of persecution. By it she was brought into intimate relationship with her suffering Saviour. Then, persecution renders another important service. It not only makes for a more Christlike Church by bringing her into a closer fellowship with Jesus, but it also serves to drive away the triflers and the cowards. It repels those who are not willing to pay the price. The writer of the Acts says in one place: "And of the rest durst no man join himself to them." That is, this persecuted Church had a repelling power as well as an attracting power. It appealed to those of heroic heart, but it frightened the rest away. There was a real gain in that. It would be a real gain in our own day.

3. Then, persecution is a roadway to a larger usefulness. That is true because, as stated above, it brings a larger purity and a closer intimacy with

God. The surest way to do more is to be more. The great awakenings of the past have not been begun by the gathering in of the many, but by the deeper consecration of the few.

Then, persecution makes for usefulness because it is one of the most effective methods of broadcasting the truth. When I was a small boy my brother and I set fire to an old dry stump that stood in the center of a grassy field. Father did not want this grass burned. But, by and by, a spark blew out and set it on fire. We organized ourselves into a fire department and began to fight the blaze. Each of us had the branch of a tree, and we fought with great zeal. We put out the fire at the spot we were fighting it, but every time we raised our weapons above our heads we scattered it to other parts of the field. The result was that all the grass was burned, to say nothing of the fence that shut it in. "Behold, how great a matter a little fire kindleth!"

Once in the city of Jerusalem there was a handful of saints who by the grace of God were incarnating these beatitudes. Suddenly persecution swept down upon them. The Jewish hierarchy, backed by the power of Rome, sent them flying from the city. "But they that were scattered abroad went everywhere preaching the Word." Instead of putting out the little blaze that had been started in Jerusalem by their persecution, they only helped them to set the world on fire. And that conflagration is burning to this good hour.

THE PERSECUTED

This, then, is the appeal of Jesus. He calls upon us to share his nature, to be like himself. He does not base his appeal on promises of exemption from battle. He is finely frank with us. He will allow no man to follow him without giving that man to understand something of the difficulties involved. He tells us openly that to be a Christian is to meet opposition. But if we dare face the opposition our reward will be great. It will be great in this present world. It will bring us deeper spiritual life and richer usefulness. It will enable us to rejoice with those of old because, for his sake, we, too, are counted worthy to suffer shame. By and by it will enable us to feel at home among those "who have come up out of great tribulation, and washed their robes, and made them white in the blood of the lamb."

> 'The Son of God goes forth to war,
>   A kingly crown to gain:
> His blood-red banner streams afar;
>   Who follows in his train?
> Who best can drink his cup of woe,
>   Triumphant over pain,
> Who patient bears his cross below,
>   He follows in his train.
>
> The martyr first, whose eagle eye
>   Could pierce beyond the grave,
> Who saw his Master in the sky,
>   And called on him to save:
> Like him, with pardon on his tongue,
>   In midst of mortal pain,
> He prayed for them that did the wrong:
>   Who follows in his train?

THE SERMON ON THE MOUNT

A glorious band, the chosen few
  On whom the Spirit came,
Twelve valiant saints, their hope they knew,
  And mocked the cross and flame;
They climbed the steep ascent of heaven
  Through peril, toil, and pain:
O God, to us may grace be given
  To follow in their train."

IX

"SALT"

Matthew 5: 13

"Ye are the salt of the earth: but if the salt have lost its savour, wherewith shall it be salted? It is thenceforth good for nothing, but to be cast out, and to be trodden under the foot of men."

I

Jesus is speaking primarily to his own disciples. He is speaking to those who have left all to follow him. Those who are the salt of the earth are the men and women who through poverty of spirit have entered into the kingdom. They are the meek and the merciful. They are the peacemakers, and those who through purity of heart have come into possession of a redeeming and transforming vision of God. But since Christ's invitation is to every man, since every man may enter the kingdom if he is willing, Christ is also speaking to the multitude. He is telling them that they, too, if they are willing, may become the salt of the earth.

"Ye are the salt of the earth." If this is taken as a declaration of our privileges, it flings a bow of hope athwart our skies beautiful and alluring beyond our dreams. If it is taken as a declaration of our obligations and responsibilities, it becomes an epitome of all the commandments and a summing up of the whole duty of man. If it is taken as a statement of fact, as it surely is, it becomes the highest of all compliments. We so recognize it to this hour. In every community there are certain characters of outstanding worth. When we want to describe such a character we say: "He is the salt of the earth." That is the highest compliment we can give. No finer could be given even by Jesus himself.

II

"Ye are the salt of the earth." Jesus is here telling us of the influence that the type of personality described by these beatitudes is to have upon the world. He is indicating the high vocation of those who possess Christlike character. He says that they are to be the salt of the earth. What does he mean by this?

1. He means that Christian character is a positive force in the world. Salt is something that cannot be ignored. It is a positive quantity. If it is present, one must recognize it. If it is absent, it is certain to be missed. It is the antithesis of the negative and the neutral. It is the sworn antagonist of the insipid. When it comes to town, folks are sure to find it out. When it leaves, they are certain to miss it. Sometimes its presence is exceedingly welcome. At other times it is keenly resented, but always it must be recognized.

Some months ago I was invited to dine in a very

lovely home. The dinner was a great success till we came to the dessert. There we came face to face with calamity. The waiter brought in some most delicious-looking, homemade ice cream. It required great self-restraint to wait till all the guests were served before tasting it. At last we were ready. The hostess began, but her brows were at once puckered into a frown. "I am so sorry," she said at once, "but you cannot eat your cream. It is full of salt." But why, I wonder, did she not keep the matter a secret? Why did she not say to herself, "A little salt will not hurt my guests; therefore I will not spoil the feast by telling them that something is wrong"? She knew that that salt would speak for itself. And so it did. It literally shrieked. She could no more quiet it than she could quiet her small boy.

Now, Jesus tells us, Christians are, in a measure, like that. They are not mere moral minus signs. They are not harmless nonentities. They are not uninteresting creatures who are "faultily faultless, icily regular, splendidly null." They are positive, pungent, strengthful folks. You may like them or dislike them, you may love them or hate them, you may fight with them or fight against them, but you cannot ignore them. Jesus was like that. Wherever he went dullness took to its heels and stagnation fled in deadly fear. Some loved him with a love that nothing could kill. Others hated him with a hatred that would not endure his being on the earth.

But wherever he went he divided men into excited groups. He simply could not be ignored.

2. Now, since salt is a positive something, it gives taste to whatever it touches. It gives piquancy to all of our feasts. Any dinner would be a most insipid affair without salt. Salt is a luxury. But it is far more than that. For civilized men it is a positive necessity. We can, if we must, get on without beautiful carpets on our floors. We can get on without lovely pictures on our walls. We can manage somehow without high-powered cars. We can, in case of absolute necessity, get on without the movies. In fact, should the worst come to the worst, we might find life very livable without a great many commodities that we now feel that we just must have. But there is one commonplace something that we cannot get on without. That something is salt. It is at once a luxury and a necessity.

And Jesus ranks himself and those who are like him among the necessities of life. Christlike character may be regarded by some as a luxury. But it is more; it is a necessity. Without it the feast of life loses its tang. How dull and stale the world had grown when Jesus came!

> "On that hard pagan world disgust
>   And secret loathing fell,
>   Deep weariness and sated lust
>   Made human life a hell."

Life always grows stale and dead without him and

those who are like him. It has no richness, no depth of meaning. It becomes a mere

> "tale told by an idiot,
> Full of sound and fury,
> Signifying nothing."

Jesus must break in upon us in order for life to thrill with lofty meaning and sing with deathless hopes. Those who regard Christians as mere incarnate insipidities that take the joy out of life are the farthest possible from the truth. On the contrary, they are the ones without whose presence the anchor soon drags, and life inevitably loses its tang.

3. Then salt is a preventive. It is the open enemy of decay. It is the foe of impurity. It is the avowed antagonist of rottenness and disintegration. It stands in the presence of the corruption, of the impurity, of the decay that so persistently lay siege to all things here and say: "They shall not pass." It purifies and sweetens and keeps sound all with which it comes in contact.

"And Christians are like that," says Jesus proudly. Without the presence of those who are Christlike, civilization does not climb upward, but goes downward. Society does not become more and more pure, but tends rather toward moral rottenness and decay. The presence of Christlike character in the world is an absolute essential if the world is to be kept from disintegration. No nation is made safe by its natural resources, its geographical position, its standing army, or by its navy. It is only made safe by the character of its people.

That is what Elisha meant when he shouted that rather startling word after Elijah. You remember how those two prophets did that last mile together before they reached the little station where God sent his own private chariot to meet Elijah. At last they have come to the parting of the ways. Elijah is being carried up into heaven. Elisha looks after him and shouts: "My father, my father, the horsemen of Israel, and the chariots thereof." What did he mean? He meant to say: "Yonder goes the defender of this nation. Yonder goes the one who, above all others, has stood between Israel and ruin." Some had been blind enough to believe that Israel's safety was in her diplomacy, in her army, in her war chariots. But her real standing army wore a prophet's mantle and tramped about the country calling men back to God. And it is my conviction at this hour that one man of Christlike character is worth more in the real defense of the world than any battleship that was ever built, or all of them together.

Saintly character is the supreme safeguard of the world. Every great disaster that has come to our race has come because there was a lack of this saving salt. There was a preacher of righteousness once who had something to say about a coming flood. But Noah did not preach the flood as inevitable. He declared that it was inevitable if men did not repent; therefore he called to his fellows to bring to bear the saving salt of saintly lives upon a world that was rotting down. They refused to hear; therefore disintegration continued to the point of final disaster. But the real tragedy of the flood was not that a certain generation ceased to live. It was, rather, the fact that that generation had ceased to be fit to live.

I have no doubt that Sodom was quite a busy and thriving city. It was buying and selling and boasting and rotting, all at the same time. Had one gone to the Chamber of Commerce and suggested that they try to induce a few men like Abraham to move down into the city to save it from moral corruption, he would doubtless have been laughed at for his pains. But that was by far the most pressing need of the city. We are informed beyond the shadow of a doubt that ten good men could have so salted the city as to have saved it. But these were not to be found. Therefore its destruction was inevitable.

Before the outbreak of the French Revolution, France became very short on the saving salt of saintly lives. Many laughed and quaffed and said: "After us the deluge." And the deluge came. It was a deluge of blood and tears. Certain historians tell us that England was on the verge of a like revolution. But somehow the tragedy was averted. Somehow this great nation did not slip into that awful abyss. Why not? It was not saved by its army and navy. It was not saved by its diplomats.

There was a man who had his heart strangely warmed in a little service in Aldersgate Street, London. That man came out from that service to bring to bear the saving salt of his transformed personality upon the masses of England, and the nation was not only saved from revolution, but it was reborn to a new moral and spiritual life.

III

Notice next the sphere of our activities. If we are salt, where are we to unloose our preventive and purifying powers?

The Master does not say that we are to salt heaven. No doubt there will be great tasks for us to do over there, but that is not the matter of which Jesus is speaking here. Nor are we to salt some far-off yesterday. There are those who exercised all their preserving and purifying powers years ago. We were genuine salt in the old home Church, but, sad to say, we are doing nothing now. Nor are we to salt some ideal situation in some to-morrow that never comes. "Ye are the salt of the earth." That is, we are to exercise our sweetening and preserving and purifying powers in the here and now. It is not an ideal sphere, maybe, but it is the only one so far as we are concerned. It gives us our one privilege for serving and lays upon us our one big responsibility.

It is our business to serve as salt in our community. It is our business, as far as in us lies, to see that our city is a clean city. We are to see to it that its atmosphere is such as will give the boys and girls the best possible chance to grow up into clean and wholesome manhood and womanhood. We are to see to it that it is as free as possible from those temptations that blight and damn. To this end we are to be ourselves Christian citizens. To this end we are to give our moral and political support to such men as stand for decency and law enforcement. We are to be relentless foes, politically, of those who violate the law or make it easy for others to do so.

We are to serve as saving salt in our own Church. This is a day in which it is especially fashionable to stone the Church. Her critics are numerous, and their voices are loud and full of clamor for attention. Nor can anyone claim that the Church is altogether blameless. It is not perfect, because it is made up of imperfect people. Yet it is doing more to salt down our present civilization and to keep it from rotting than any other institution in the world. It is doing more to safeguard those fundamental integrities on which civilization rests than all other institutions combined. Many a man who has his own life and the lives of those he loves safeguarded by it makes no better returns than that of cheap and sometimes ignorant criticism. Kipling's rebuke to those who ridiculed England's peace-time army seems to fit in here:

> "Making fun of uniforms
> That guard you while you sleep,
> Is cheaper than them uniforms,
> And that's starvation cheap."

Nor is it fair to judge the Church solely by its positive accomplishments, though, judged according to that measure, its benefits are incalculable. Every other institution that I know that is exercising the lifting power of an ounce receives its inspiration from the Church. But we need to judge the Church also in the light of what it prevents. Our city is not what it ought to be, but how much worse would it be without the Church! We ourselves are not all that we ought to be, but how much worse would we likely be without the influence of the Church! A young chap presented me with a check some years ago, saying that he had forged it. His comment was this: "I did not cash that check this morning because I heard you preach last night." Sometimes there are services that seem very meager in positive results. But we can never really know what was accomplished. We can certainly never know how many were fortified and strengthened and kept from falling.

But granting that the Church is not what it should be, what is your remedy? Do you expect to cure it by letting it alone? Do you expect to cure it by ignoring it? Do you expect to cure it by throwing stones at it? Or, do you propose to bring to its languishing life that saving salt of a Christlike personality? Years ago I went to serve a Church that was torn to shreds by internal strife. "The devil has this Church," a man said one day. But a certain old saint overheard the remark and answered: "He hasn't got my seat yet. I am in it myself every service, and I am going to see to it that he does not get it." And that man became a rallying point round which God wrought a great victory.

Then, we are to salt our own homes. That is the surest way to salt the Church. That is the surest way to salt the world. If we really bring to bear the saving salt of saintly character in our own homes we shall thereby help to salt our nation. We shall thereby sooner or later help to salt every nation in the wide world. And the world will never be salted any other way. A man may be born again when he is old, but, comparatively, it is a rare miracle. The longer I live, the more I come to realize that the only sure way to have Christians is to raise them. If we bring to bear the saving salt of Christlikeness upon our children in their young and tender years, we shall not only save them for heaven, but we shall save them for this world as well. How many have been brought back from lives of sin by the memory of a godly father and mother! How far many more have been prevented from going into sin by these same precious memories! "I could not do it," said a certain young chap as he faced a sordid temptation, "because I remembered my mother." How often is it so!

> "Her voice is heard through roaring drums
>   That beat to battle where he stands:
> Her face across his fancy comes,
>   And gives the battle to his hands."

IV

Then, if we are to salt the earth, how is it to be

done? What is the method that Jesus here suggests? Two words give the answer. We are to salt through character and contact.

1. We are the salt of the earth by being Christlike. Jesus did not say: "You are to scatter salt." He said: "Ye are salt." If we are to save the world, it must be through the compelling power of saintly character. It is important to do, but to be is of supreme and fundamental importance. I cannot help to salt the earth unless I have salt in myself. If the Christian loses his enthusiasm, if he loses his tang, if he becomes insipid, then he becomes utterly useless. He is fit for nothing but to be thrown away.

We can easily understand why this is true. Moffatt makes the author of the one hundred and nineteenth Psalm say: "I hate men that are half and half." With that sentiment we all agree. With that sentiment Christ agrees. There is no type of character that he finds quite so repellent as the half-hearted. That was the trouble with the Church at Laodicea. It had lost its zeal. It had lost its glow. Its enthusiasms were dead. It had become dull, listless, insipid, mere savorless salt. No wonder Jesus said: "I would thou wert cold or hot. So then because thou art lukewarm, and neither cold nor hot, I will spew thee out of my mouth." If we hope to salt the world, we must shun insipidity as we shun the very pangs of hell.

Then, if we are to salt the earth we must come into contact with those whom we are to salt. When we used to kill our meat on the farm, I often assisted at the salting. We did not salt meat by putting the salt in one barrel and the meat in another. The two had to be brought into contact. Not only was the salt given to the meat, but that salt lost itself in a sense by that giving. It passed out of sight altogether. It saved the meat at the expense of itself. It could not possibly save in any other way.

And the same law holds good for you and me. If we are to bring to bear the saving salt of a saintly life upon the world, it is going to be costly. It was so for Jesus. When he set out to save the world, he did not undertake the task while keeping himself at a distance. He came into contact with men in the most intimate fashion possible. He knew no cheaper way than the laying down of his life. "The Son of Man came not to be ministered unto, but to minister, and to give his life a ransom for many." And it is enough for the servant that he be as his Lord. We can serve in no other way. To be unwilling to bleed is to be incapacitated to bless. "Except a corn of wheat fall into the ground and die, it abideth alone; but if it die, it bringeth forth much fruit."

X

LIGHT

Matthew 5: 14-16

"Ye are the light of the world. A city that is set on a hill cannot be hid. Neither do men light a candle, and put it under a bushel, but on a candlestick; and it giveth light unto all that are in the house. Let your light so shine before men, that they may see your good works, and glorify your Father which is in heaven."

I

"Ye are the light of the world." Here again our Lord is giving us his conception of the Christian life. To be a Christian is to be a light-bringer. What a thrilling and breath-taking word! Last Sunday we said that when Jesus called us salt he paid us the highest possible compliment. But it is certainly no higher than this. In fact, in saying, "Ye are the light of the world," he couples our names with his own in a way that is perfectly amazing. For he who said, "Ye are the light of the world," is the One who said: "I am the Light of the world."

Of course there is this vast difference between his light and ours. Our Lord is light in himself. When the prophets dreamed of him they saw him as the bringer of a new day. He was to rise on a darkened world as the Sun of Righteousness with healing in his wings. He is the true light that, coming into the world, lighteth every man. We shine only as we are touched and transformed by himself. If he dwells with us, we shine through him. But apart from him we can do nothing. The moment we lose contact the light goes out.

It was Paul who said: "For me to live is Christ." He might have said with equal truth: "For me to shine is Christ." So we also may say. That distant planet that keeps eternal lids apart in the night sky says: "For me to shine is the sun." Not that all the light of the sun is centered in that one star, but all the light it has and gives comes from the sun. Buffalo, N. Y., is lighted by the power that comes from Niagara Falls. Every light that blazes in that city says: "For me to shine is Niagara." Not that all the power of that thundering cataract is expended on that one light, but whatever power it has comes from Niagara. Apart from that power it could not shine. Apart from Christ we cannot shine.

II

But if we know Jesus, if we are possessors of the kingdom, we are light. Being light, we can shine. That is our business. That is what we are lighted for. Of course Christ has a purpose in our salvation that reaches beyond ourselves. He wants every man to know him because of the transforming power of that knowledge and the joy it brings to the man himself. But no man is saved simply and solely for himself. No lamp is ever lighted just for its own benefit. It is lighted in order to give light. That is true of ourselves. Since it is true, how are we to shine?

1. We are to shine naturally. That is what any real light will do. How did this rose become so red? What rouge does it use? It uses none at all. Its nature is to be red. Why does the ocean sprawl so broad and wide between the continents? Why does it boom its perpetual cannonade along all shores? It does so naturally. Why does that mountain climb so high that it has to wrap a mantel of shimmering whiteness around its shoulders even during the hottest days of summer? It is not standing on tiptoe. It is naturally tall. Why does that bird sing as if the whole world were listening? It is not putting on a show; it is the nature of that bird to sing.

And if we are light in the Lord, we are going to shine naturally. There is going to be a beautiful spontaneity about our radiance. There was once a gifted and fascinating young man who was being mobbed. The stones were flying thick about him. But the stones could not banish the light that shone upon his face. "They saw his face as it had been the face of an angel." He did not make his face bright of set purpose. His fellowship with God made that brightness natural to him. Looking unto him, he became radiant with a radiance that those who beheld him could not fail to recognize. Paul saw it, and it haunted him till it brought him to Christ.

Peter and John were arrested one day. The court

that tried them gave them very strict orders. They were not to speak any more nor teach in the name of Jesus. But what was their answer? It was very clear and emphatic. "We cannot but speak the things we have seen and heard." "What you command," they say, "is utterly impossible. We are light, and, being light, we cannot but shine. We have a story that is far too good to keep. Were we resolved to do so, the Word would be as a burning fire shut up in our bones. Being light, we cannot but give light to those that sit in darkness."

2. Not only are we to shine naturally, but we are to shine willingly and of set purpose. We are to shine sacrificially. Shining is natural for light, but it is always costly. Wherever you see a light you may know that something is being burned up. You may know that energy is being expended. As the candle burns, it grows shorter and shorter. As the lamp burns, it consumes not only the oil, but the wick as well. And even though it is electricity that is burning in that globe, by and by we shall have to throw the globe away because it will be burned out. When Jesus came as the Light of the world, his shining was infinitely costly. The disciples received a hint of the price he was paying when they looked into his tired, spent face. The very weariness they recognized brought them the interpretation of a text they had not understood before. They said: "The zeal for God's house is burning him up." Jesus said of John that he was a burning and a shining light. So he was. But if you will take a glance

into that gloomy prison cell, if you will look at that severed head that is now glutting the vengeance of that hard-faced woman, you will realize something of the price he paid. Shining is expensive even when God supplies the power, for the wick must burn with the oil.

3. Then, we are to shine openly. We are to shine before men. That is not always easy. There are some who are not friendly to light. Jesus knew such in his day. "Some men," he tells us, "love darkness rather than light, because their deeds are evil." When a criminal sets out to do a crime, he does not welcome the light. He desires that the shadows be as black as possible. Lady Macbeth did not look for the light as she purposed and planned the murder of Duncan. She rather said:

> 'Come, thick night,
> And pall thee in the dunnest smoke of hell,
> That my keen knife see not the wound it makes,
> Nor heaven peep through the blanket of the dark
> To cry, 'Hold, hold!'"

When the Bastille was stormed, those engaged in the task came to one dark cell where the light had not shone for long years. They battered down the door, let in a flood of sunshine, and invited the prisoner to come out to freedom. But he shrank back and covered his eyes and begged them to shut the door to keep out the light. So long had he lived in the dark that light had become painful to him. Did you ever turn over a rotting log in the forest and see the creatures of the dark that were hidden under

LIGHT

it? How the light troubled and frightened them! If you could have heard them, I think they would have been saying; "Put out the light." And there are those in every age that shrink from the light that flashes from the face of Christ or from the life of one illuminated by the light of Christ.

But we are not for this reason to leave off our shining. We are not for this reason to put our lights under a bushel. We are not to be afraid to be openly Christian We are not to be afraid to be ourselves. Dr. Sockman spoke recently of "The New Hypocrisy." He declared that there was a day when the Church was strong and dominant in the life of the people; that, in that day, to win popularity men often sought to appear better than they were. That was the old hypocrisy. To-day, when the Church does not loom so large in the public eye, there are those who seek to appear worse than they are. That is the new hypocrisy.

And this new hypocrisy is altogether too common. How many are afraid to appear as good as they actually are! They are ashamed of the convictions that they possess. They are ashamed to acknowledge the faith that is very dear to them. They are ashamed of the ideals that are the very glory of their manhood and womanhood. This same speaker referred to a conversation that he overheard in the smoking room on a train. A group of fairly clean-faced men were talking. From their conversation one would have thought that every one of the group had his private bootlegger and that every one spent all his leisure time in the lowest night clubs of New York. If we have been lighted by the power of God, let us not hide our light under the bushel of cowardice.

Then we must avoid hiding our light under the bushel of inconsistency or positive sin. I once had a most earnest worker in my Church. There was scarcely any task that she was not willing to undertake. I have seen her serve sacrificially for hours and even days, till her light was shining with beautiful radiance. Then she would turn down a bushel of temper over it and put it almost absolutely out. In the little church that I attended as a boy the brother who led the singing at night used to hold a lamp in his hand with which to beat time and, incidentally, to help him to see. But too often he would tilt the lamp to such an angle that the chimney was soon so blackened that the light was dimmed. A lamp to shine its best must stand upright. The same is true of ourselves. We cannot shine before men if we are not morally and spiritually erect.

4. Then, we must shine where we are. This is one glory of light, that it is democratic. When the sun rose this morning it illuminated the pigsty with the same radiance that it spilled upon the flower garden. It shone upon the clean and the unclean with equal brightness. A candle will shine just as beautifully in a poor man's cottage as in a rich man's palace. It will shine just as brightly in the most obscure corner of the earth as upon the steps of a throne. And if we

are going to light the world we must do so by shining where we are. There is not much poetry, but plenty of excellent sense, in that popular song, "Brighten the Corner Where You Are." If you do not shine where you are, then you will not shine at all. I don't know what your candlestick is. It may be some conspicuous place. It may be a high social position. It may be a prominent place in the business world. It may be the platform of a popular pulpit. Or it may be a very obscure place. It may be a humble home. It may even be no larger than a sick bed. But whatever it is, and wherever it is, there you are to shine. It is your one chance.

It is by our thus shining where we are that the world's night is to be banished. For it is as we shine individually that we are to add to the sum total of the world's light. It is by each individual shining that the Church comes to be as a city set upon a hill. That city upon the hill that cannot be hid is not made up of just one individual. It is composed of many. In the pioneer days when the saints set out for the night service, each carried a candle. One candle did very little toward making the house bright. But all the candles brought the needed light and made the service possible. So as each shines in his own place the shadows are to flee away, and the new day is to come.

III

Now, if we thus shine, Jesus has no slightest doubt as to the beneficent results that will follow.

He says that such shining will be victorious, that such shining will conquer the night. He says that such shining will result not in applause for ourselves; that is not what we are seeking if we are Christians. It will result in the salvation of men and in their giving glory to God. The reasons for this are very obvious. Such results are but the natural outcome of light. This is true for the following reasons:

1. Light is a positive something. Wherever light shines it is going to be seen. That is absolutely sure. If nobody sees our light, it is certainly for one of two reasons. It is because we have no light, or because we have hidden it away under some kind of bushel. Light, just as salt, is something that cannot be ignored. Black night might say: "I am not going to pay a bit of attention to the sun. I am not going to give an inch." But in spite of its boasting when the sun comes it takes to its heels. Light is positive, and the positive forces win.

2. Then, light is cheering and comforting. There is something depressing about darkness. It is the symbol of the sorrowful and the mysterious. There is something frightening about it. In the dark one can see anything that a fevered imagination suggests. The most familiar object can easily become a distorted monstrosity. It is not to be wondered at that when John dreamed of heaven he thought of it as a land of light and said: "There shall be no night there." I think I have never been much given to fear, but when I hear things about the house in the

late hours of the night, I love the light. There is something cheering and consoling about it.

And how cheering and consoling is this light that flashes from the face of Christ! "Be of good cheer" is a word that was on his lips again and again. He said it in the presence of the fury of nature. He said it in the presence of the ravages of sin. He said it in the presence of the mystery and tragedy of death. These glooms are about us still. We all need the light to shine into our darkness. We need to be delivered from the fear of yesterday and the fear of to-morrow. We need to see life illuminated by the light of God. We need to see death, not as a blind alley that leads to oblivion, but as a wide-open roadway into our Father's house.

3. Light awakens. A few hours ago the world was asleep. The sheep and the cattle were lying down in the pastures. The birds had their heads tucked under their wings, except here and there an enthusiastic mocker who, having to sing all the songs in the birds' hymn book, must needs turn night into day. But now all our world is awake. How did it come about? Did God turn loose a million alarm clocks? Did he shake the birds out of the trees? No. He just lifted the sun above the eastern hills, and the multitudinous life of the world awakened and began a new day.

When Christianity was born, it was night. Almost the whole world was in the grip of a common religion, the religion of polytheism, which was a religion of shadows. But the preaching of these early disciples awakened the world and brought in a new day. When the Church forgot her high task and hid her lamp under a bushel, then came the Dark Ages. There were a thousand years of night. Then Martin Luther came into vital contact with the Light of the World. Through the light that blazed from his hot heart and radiant face there came a great awakening. Through the centuries Christian character has been an awakening power.

4. Light makes for health. It is at once a preventive and a cure. It tends to shut the door in the face of invading disease, or to cast it out if it has already entered. It makes incessant war against the friends of sickness and gives help to the friends of health. A house physician in a London hospital declared that it took a simple fracture from seven to fourteen days longer to heal in a certain dark ward of the hospital than in another that was well lighted. Unsunned places are ever the abodes of weakness, sickness, and degeneracy. It is our high task as Christians so to shine as to help bring light to all that sit in darkness. In so doing we shall do our part toward bringing health and healing to our sick and disordered world.

5. Finally, light reveals. Light enables us to see. A face of beauty is no fairer than one of ugliness if we have no light. It is in the radiance of the light of Christ that we see ourselves. It is in the radiance of this light that we see our possibilities. Old Born Drunk, in "Twice-Born Men," had never known a sober day. He had been made drunk at his mother's

breast. Few, indeed, imagined that he could ever be different. But one day he looked into the face of Joe, who had once been almost as low as himself, but who had been wonderfully transformed. At once he began to dream that there was hope for himself. "All at once," he declared, "it came home to me that I might be like Joe." From that hour Old Born Drunk began to walk in newness of life. From that hour he became a shining light in his sordid world.

It is by the light of Christian character that we get a vision of the face of God. That is why Jesus came as the Light of the world. He came to show us God. He revealed to us God's infinite loveliness as the world had never seen it before. He showed us that God was our Father. The Psalmists had come close to him, but they had never come close enough to discover that fact. And what higher vocation can you and I possibly dream of than just this, to live such lives day by day that those who come in contact with us will see in the radiance of our lives something of the loveliness of God, that they will discover that God is our Father and theirs? Making this discovery, they will surely glorify our Father who is in heaven.

XI

FULFILLING THE LAW

Matthew 5: 17-48

By the time the Young Prophet had reached this part of his sermon his audience was on tiptoe of expectation. They were wondering whether he was a radical or a conservative. Had he broken with the old religion as, in a measure, John the Baptist had done, John who never went to the temple and never offered sacrifices? Or was he still loyal to the faith of his fathers? Each group was listening eagerly for an answer to these questions just as a present-day audience might listen for some catchword that would indicate whether the speaker was a fundamentalist or a modernist.

Jesus soon made his position clear. "Think not that I am come to destroy the law and the prophets." He disclaimed at once the rôle of an iconoclast. He is no mere destructionist. Naturally not. No man was ever sent of God to do nothing but destroy. To tear down, to wreck, requires little either of heart or of brains. An idiot can destroy more in an hour than a great artist could build in a score of years. Jesus, therefore, is not here as a mere destroyer. What is essential in the law is going to abide. "One jot or one tittle shall in no wise pass till all be fulfilled."

What, then, is to be his attitude to the law? He is here to fulfill it, to perfect it, to bring it to completion. When a youth passes from high school to college, he does not do so to destroy what he has learned in his earlier years. He is undertaking to carry the knowledge already acquired further toward completion. When the soil and the sunshine and the rain lay hold of an acorn, they do not destroy it. They bring it to its completion in the giant oak. Thus Jesus fulfills the law. The old law was good, but it was not perfect. It was of value, but it was not complete. Had it been so, we should not have needed the work of Jesus.

And with what a kingly stride he goes about the task, with what superb assurance, with what majestic audacity! "Ye have heard that it was said by them of old time, . . . but I say unto you." This he repeats again and again. Who are these who spoke of old time? They are the prophets. They are men who spoke as they were moved of the Spirit. They are men, therefore, of great authority. They begin their messages, and rightly, with this big declaration: "Thus saith the Lord." But this Young Prophet appeals to no authority other than himself. He speaks in his own name. "But I say unto you." Thus he speaks as only he has a right to speak in whom are hidden all the treasures of wisdom and knowledge. He speaks as one who can say: "He that hath seen me hath seen the Father."

I

How, then, does Jesus fulfill the law?

1. He fulfills the law in his own person. That is not the point emphasized in this sermon, but it is true none the less. It became him to fulfill all righteousness. The law found its complete fulfillment in him.

2. He fulfills the law by giving it a greater inwardness. Before his coming the law had to do largely with the outside of life. It concerned itself with conduct. Its attention was fixed on the flying wheels of action. Jesus takes us down into the power house. He takes us into the engine room. He shows us the dynamo. He takes us into the hidden chambers of the heart. He knows that one is not always known by his actions. To really know a man we must visit the inner chambers of thought and imagination. We must hear him dream and see him think. For, "as a man thinketh in his heart, so is he."

3. Jesus gave to the law a new positiveness. He made it constructive. Before his coming it consisted largely of prohibitions. Its predominant word was: "Thou shalt not." There were so many things that one was not allowed to do that there was little time for positive doing. Jesus changed the emphasis. He said: "Except your goodness exceeds the goodness of the scribes and Pharisees, ye shall in no case enter into the kingdom of heaven." He focused our attention, not upon what we are not

FULFILLING THE LAW

to be, but what we are to be. He emphasized, not what we are forbidden to do, but what we are to do. Every parable of judgment that he uttered was against those guilty of failure in duty rather than against those who had violated some definite law. Goodness, according to Jesus, is not an absence of faults, but the presence of positive virtues.

II

The remainder of this chapter is taken up with illustrations of how Christ fulfills the law. I am not going to take these illustrations in their order.

1. Look at the seventh commandment. "Ye have heard that it was said by them of old time, Thou shalt not commit adultery." Nothing was forbidden but the act of sin. "But I say unto you, Whosoever looketh on a woman to lust after her hath committed adultery with her already in his heart." The word translated "to" here means in order to. The one condemned is the one who has a deliberate purpose to sin. His intentions are all in that direction. He only fails to carry out those intentions because of fear or because he cannot. His intention, his will being toward the wrong, the man himself is wrong. The intention is taken for the deed.

Now, what is true of the seventh commandment is true of every other. Sin homes in the will. The man who wills to come to Christ is a Christian. The man who wills to sin is a sinner, whether the thought and purpose of his heart are ever translated into act or not. The man who refuses to steal simply because he fears detection is a thief. The man who is honest simply because honesty is the best policy is really not honest at all. "Thou shalt not commit adultery," said the law. "Thou shalt be clean in thy thoughts and in thy purposes," said Jesus.

2. "It hath been said, Whosoever shall put away his wife, let him give her a writing of divorcement." This was the law. It was some protection for the divorced woman. But it was very incomplete. It was exceedingly imperfect. About all a husband had to do who wanted to be rid of his wife was to give her a statement saying, "Whereas this woman was once my wife, she is now mine no more." He could then send her on away and still be fully within the law.

But how vastly Jesus deepened and widened this law, and how much of purity and of decency and of moral uplift the world owes to that fact! He said: "For this cause shall a man leave father and mother and shall cleave unto his wife, and they twain shall be one flesh. What, therefore, God hath joined together, let not man put asunder." That is, marriage is a divine institution. It is for life. There is but one valid reason for divorce, and that is adultery. This is a hard saying to some, I know, but the seriously regarding and obeying of it is necessary in order to keep civilization from disintegrating.

3. "Thou shalt not forswear thyself, but shall perform unto the Lord thine oaths." So spoke the law. Jesus said: "Swear not at all, . . . but let your communication be, Yea, yea; Nay, nay: for whatso-

FULFILLING THE LAW

ever is more than these cometh of evil." Now, what Jesus is forbidding here is not the taking of a legal oath. He himself accepted a legal oath on one occasion, as we see in Matthew 26. He is commanding us to tell the plain, unvarnished truth, to be genuinely sincere. Thus he is laying down a law so wide and deep that an oath becomes superfluous. It becomes utterly unnecessary. "Tell the truth. Be truly honest, and you will have no need to swear."

Now, it is a fact that a genuinely honest man does not need an oath in order to make him truthful. If a man is truly sincere in the inner deeps of his soul, he will speak the truth without any oath. In fact, I am convinced that the man who will lie when not under oath will also lie if he is under oath. The taking of an oath becomes a positive evil when it leads one to believe that lying is less hurtful and less wrong when no oath is taken.

This was the horrible situation into which the habit of swearing had plunged the people to whom Jesus was speaking. They did not believe the obligation to tell the truth was binding at all except under oath. They did not believe that all oaths were binding. One might swear by heaven or by earth or by his head and get away with it. Thus lying had become a veritable plague among them. They had the greatest number of oaths and were about the most prolific liars in the world. And lying hurts the liar. It is also a menace to the social order. No wonder, therefore, that Jesus did not say, "Do not violate your oath," but passed on to the higher ground and said: "Tell the truth and make oath-taking absolutely unnecessary."

4. Then there are three striking illustrations that have to do with the treatment of our fellows. They have especially to do with the treatment of those with whom for one reason or another we are tempted to be at enmity.

(1) There was the law against killing. "Thou shalt not kill." To keep this law one had only to refrain from striking his brother dead. His attitude toward him was not taken into consideration at all. Jesus pushed the law back into those depths where murder is born. He forbade us to be angry with our brother without cause. There is a question as to whether or not "without cause" belongs in the text. Personally, I think it has a right there. I think so because there are times when anger is altogether just and right. We must believe this or discredit our Master.

For instance, one day Jesus went into the temple, where he found a man with a withered hand. This man had a heavy handicap. He was not playing his part in the world of men as he might have played it. But there were certain religious leaders present who were far more concerned about their petty regulations than they were about the man's cure. And we read that Jesus looked round about upon them with anger. It was an anger that scorched and blistered and burned. But it was not born of any injury that these religionists had done to Jesus himself. It was not selfish, as ours so often is. It was born of love.

And such anger becomes at times not only a right, but a positive duty.

But what Jesus is forbidding here is selfish and vindictive anger. And this is the type of anger with which we are tragically familiar. We meet it in ourselves and others. Such anger is wrong. It is incipient murder. The difference between the selfishly angry man who does not strike and him who actually kills is in degree rather than kind. Therefore to be thus angry is to be guilty. To allow that anger to lead to words of contempt, as "Raca, you common fellow," is to be more guilty still. To allow it to lead to terms of abuse, as "Thou fool," is to be in danger of the very severest punishment.

But not only are we forbidden to be angry and contemptuous and abusive. These are merely negative. We are to do our best to make up with our brother, to get on good terms with him. This is of supreme importance. It even comes before worship, for without it real worship is impossible. "Therefore, if thou bring thy gift to the altar, and there rememberest that thy brother hath aught against thee; leave there thy gift before the altar, and go thy way; first be reconciled to thy brother, and then come and offer thy gift." Our singing, our giving, our praying—these will all come to little if we have an unbrotherly attitude toward any human soul.

Then, the Master gives us an extreme case. He says, if you are on your way to the court and meet your adversary, do your best to come to terms of friendship with him, try to settle the matter out of court. If you do not, he may turn you over to the judge, and the judge to the officer, and you be cast into prison. This does not mean a literal prison, but the prison of your own anger, of your own hostility, of your own hate. I have known many in such prisons. There may be some present who are locked in the gloomy dungeon of their own malice. If such is the case, let me remind you that you are in about the most wretched and ruinous prison in the world.

(2) Next, Jesus tells us how to treat those who have done us an injury or who would appeal to us for help. "Ye have heard that it was said by them of old time, An eye for an eye, and a tooth for a tooth." This was not the best possible law, but it was best for the time when it was enacted. Under this law, if you should knock my eye out, I would have the right to knock yours out. That would be justice, and no more. Without such a law, if you had knocked my eye out, I might have knocked both of yours out. If you had broken my arm, I might have broken both of yours. So this law was good, but it was not good enough. Therefore Jesus said: "But I say unto you, that you resist not evil: but whosoever shall smite thee on thy right cheek, turn to him the other also."

An arresting word, surely. Nor does it become easier as we proceed. "And if a man will sue thee at the law, and take away thy coat, let him have thy cloak also. And whosoever shall compel thee to go a mile, go with him twain. Give to him that asketh

FULFILLING THE LAW

thee, and from him that would borrow of thee, turn not thou away." Certainly this is one of the most startling utterances that ever fell from the lips of Jesus. If we interpret it in a crass and wooden and literal fashion, it brings us into a situation that is nothing short of impossible. And it is well to remember that our Lord never calls us to throw dust in the eyes of reason nor spit in the face of sanctified common sense.

Just what, then, does Jesus mean? I do not take his meaning to be that we are to give to every one who asks a gift, regardless of who the individual is or how he intends to use what we give. There are times when such giving would rob both him that gives and him that takes. I do not take it that it is never right to resist an evildoer. To fail to do so would often hurt the evildoer, his victim, and society as a whole. There was one occasion when Jesus resorted to measures that look very much like physical force. When the temple was being desecrated by a crowd of irreverent tricksters, he took a scourge of small cords and drove the whole herd out, pell-mell, and overturned their money tables.

But while there are times when resistance may be both a right and a duty, those cases are certainly exceptions. Therefore, while we are not to interpret this passage with bald literalness, we must remember that Jesus means something by it. He means something high and exacting, and he means that something most intensely. We must remember also that he was no dreamer. He was no spinner of idle and worthless theories. In taking him seriously we are sure to find the best way of life both for ourselves and for others. This is Jesus's way of treating those who did him wrong. He means for us to go and do likewise.

What is our attitude toward those who insult us? What is our attitude toward those who slap our faces, if not with their hands, then in some other fashion equally hard to bear? If one slaps my face, it is suggested that I can take either one of three courses. I can hit back. In that case the most skillful boxer wins. But nothing is decided save who is the stronger man physically. That is about all that has been decided by the wars that have billowed the continents with graves through the long centuries. Another thing I can do is to run. In that case I may save myself temporarily from personal harm, but I also encourage my antagonist in his evil ways. Again, I can refuse either to run or to fight. I can stand my ground and take his insult. I can thus demonstrate that I had rather suffer wrong than to do wrong.

This is the method of Jesus. It is one that we have tried out all too little, either individually or nationally. But it is the only one in which there is any real hope. I know a man who some years ago in the heat of discussion on a conference floor got his face slapped. He refused to hit back. There was not the slightest retaliation in any fashion. But every man knew which of the two was really courageous The aggressor on that occasion has slipped into utter oblivion. The other is one of the most influential forces for moral uplift in America to-day. The way of Jesus is not an easy way. It outrages our human nature. It requires a bigness of soul and a grandeur of courage that are truly Christlike. "When he was reviled, he reviled not again." But it is infinitely the best way both for the individual and for society.

(3) The climax is reached when Jesus commands us to love all men, whether friends or foes. What said the old law? "Thou shalt love thy neighbor." Hate for an enemy was not commanded, but it was permitted and that was enough. Therefore Jesus said: "Ye have heard that it was said, Thou shalt love thy neighbor, and hate thine enemy. But I say unto you, Love your enemies, bless them that curse you, do good to them that hate you, and pray for them which despitefully use you, and persecute you." In other words he says: "Treat your enemies as God treats his."

Now, that is just where we fail. We take publicans and pagans rather than our Lord for our example. Pagans love their own friends. They love those that are kind to them and appreciate them. We must do far more than that if we show ourselves kinfolks with God. He is not only kind to his friends, but to his enemies as well. He maketh the sun to shine upon the evil and upon the good. When the sun rose this morning it illuminated that Christian home where pious hands were folded in prayer. It also shone just as brightly upon that stenchful brothel where depraved men and women were wakening from a night of debauch. It shone upon the wheat field of the consecrated widow. It shone also upon the fields of the scoffer who denies and despises the God in whose hands his breath is and in whose are all his ways.

You see, our Lord does not retaliate. He is not spiteful. He is never after getting even with a foe. He never takes a dare. When he hung on the cross they dared him to come down. "If thou be the Son of God, save thyself." But he did not take the dare. And when a few months ago a poor misguided author took out his watch and dared him to strike him dead, he was infinitely too big to pay any attention to the poor egotist. And we are to take him as our example. We are to meet the world, not our friends only, but our foes as well, with a dauntless friendliness like that of Jesus Christ himself.

It is a high standard. It is so high that we cannot attain in our own strength. The Sermon on the Mount is said to be purely ethical. But it implies a gospel of redemption. More, it demands one. It makes the new birth an absolute necessity. These commands are even beyond the reach of us unless we become partakers of the divine nature. We cannot love according to the Sermon on the Mount except we are empowered by him whose "nature and whose name is love."

XII

DRASTIC OPERATIONS

Matthew 5: 29, 30

"If thy right eye offend thee, pluck it out. . . . .
If thy right hand offend thee, cut it off."

THESE are bold and startling words. They seem to have a decided flavor of the extreme. I wonder just what they would mean to the average man of the world were he to read them. I wonder what they actually mean to the average member of the Church. What lesson did Christ intend to teach when he spoke of the plucking out of the right eye and the cutting off of the right hand? It is very plain language. Any child can understand it. These words were easily comprehended when they were first uttered. It is even more easy to understand them, at least superficially, to-day, because surgery is now far more common than it was in the days of Christ. And these words smack of the operating room. As we hear them there comes to us the odor of ether or of gas. We catch a glimpse of the faces of the attendant physicians. We hear the soft voice of the nurse. We look into the anxious eyes of loved ones and friends. We catch the faint perfume of flowers. We shrink again at the cutting pain. We turn restlessly with a torturing nervousness and struggle with annoying nausea. All of us know either from our own experience or from that of some loved one, what it is to undergo an operation.

I

Why are operations performed?

One would almost think that their purpose was to give us a new topic of conversation. Irvin Cobb declares that since his hospital experience, whenever he meets a friend, though the subject has not even been hinted at, he opens the conversation by saying: "Speaking of operations." "Then," says he, "I am off." He proceeds to entertain his audience with his early symptoms, with the doctor's diagnosis, and he reaches a grand climax in telling of his actually going under the operation. And, truly, it is a great subject for conversation. I confess that some of the most impatient moments of my life have been spent in listening to some friend tell how he felt as he was coming from under the anæsthetic. Not that the story was not interesting, but I was eager for him to get through so I could tell how I felt when I was coming from under the anæsthetic.

But this is not the real purpose of operations. Nor are they performed solely for the entertainment of the physician and the attendant nurses. One would almost fancy at times that this is the case. Mr. Cobb said that he thought his was going to be a kind of private affair, but that he discovered

DRASTIC OPERATIONS

that the physician had invited all his friends, and that the patient had no more privacy than a gold fish. Neither do we undergo operations for our own pleasure or amusement. Possibly there were some pleasurable moments connected with your sojourn in the hospital, but the experience is not one that you would like to repeat. Most of us who have undergone operations of any degree of seriousness cannot think of the possibility of another without a dread that is often akin to terror. We think of the restless days and the sleepless nights. We recall how pain nagged at us as if it were taking a fiendish delight in our suffering. Undergoing an operation is no picnic. We should never enter upon such an experience just for the fun of it.

But why, I repeat, do we suffer operations? Sometimes we undergo an operation in order to improve our health. Our physician informs us that while our trouble might never prove fatal, yet we can never get entirely well without resorting to the knife. Therefore, in order to save ourselves from an annoying handicap, in order to avoid permanently lessening our efficiency, we consent to undergo an operation. Such operations are not matters of life and death. We suffer them because we believe that by so doing we shall be of more worth both to others and to ourselves.

Then there are times when the situation is more serious still. A man told me sometime ago of a certain gentleman who, while walking along the streets of one of our cities, seemingly in perfect health, suddenly fell to the pavement as if he had been struck by a rifle bullet. He was taken up unconscious and hurried to the hospital. An X-ray indicated that a little piece of bone was resting upon a certain very delicate part of the brain. The man might doubtless have lived for some time without the removal of that bone. But he would have lived with health impaired. He would have lived with sanity gone and, therefore, with all usefulness gone. He would have lived as a burden upon those who loved him rather than as a help. But with the removal of this bone he was restored to health.

Then there are times when an operation is essential for the saving of life. I have a friend who is one of the best specialists in America. He is a pioneer in his field. His discoveries have cost him much. His hands are horribly burned. Last year a blister came in the palm of one of his hands. The inflammation spread. At last the doctor told him that the only way to save his life was to remove that offending hand. And though the loss was a serious one, yet he underwent the operation. He threw his good hand away because he saw that if he kept it, it would mean the loss of his whole body. The purpose of operations, therefore, is the improving of health and the saving of life.

II

But when Jesus speaks the strong words of the text is he suggesting physical surgery as a preventative or as a cure for sin?

DRASTIC OPERATIONS

Does he mean that if my eyes tend to look to the impure and to the unclean the remedy is for me to pluck them out? Does he mean that if this tongue of mine is given to slander and to criticism and to profane swearing the remedy is for me to have my tongue taken out?. When the very talkative old lady told the new preacher that her one objection to him was that his coat was too long and that she would like to cut off a foot of it, was his answer wise when he suggested that her tongue was too long and that he would like to cut off a bit of that? If my hand tends to slip into the other fellow's pocket, or if it tends to knot itself into a fist to strike the other man's face, is the cure for this that I shall have my right hand cut off? I do not think so.

1. Such a remedy would be altogether ineffective. It would deal with the outside rather than with the inside. It would fail utterly in reaching the cause of the evil. When our organ gets out of tune, we do not cure the evil by polishing the pipes. When your watch ceases to keep good time, you will not cure it by treating the hands. When your well is found to be full of typhoid germs, you will not remedy the evil by painting the curb. When your car fails to run, you will not help matters by dusting the fenders or polishing the hood. No more can any operation performed on the body serve as a remedy for sin.

If this right hand of mine is constantly doing the wrong thing, the fault is not with the hand; it is with the will that backs the hand and sets it to the doing of its evil task. If these eyes of mine tend constantly to gaze into the mud rather than into the heights, if they are constantly seeking the unclean rather than the clean, it is not the fault of the eyes; it is the fault of the heart that is back of the eyes. If this tongue of mine is forever saying the unkind and the cutting and the discouraging word, the fault is not with the tongue; it is with the man that wields the tongue. When that man was killed the other day, it was not the gun that was tried for its life; it was the man who wielded the gun.

2. Not only did Jesus not suggest surgery as a remedy because such a remedy is inadequate and ineffective, but because, even were it effective, it would be purely negative. Even supposing that the cutting off of my right hand would prevent my ever stealing again, if I were a thief, that would be a very poor salvation. For, if I could never reach forth my hand again to take what was not my own, neither could I reach it forth to give. If I could not use it again for the despoiling of my brother, neither could I ever use it to lift him upon his feet. If the putting out of my eyes would prevent me from seeing what I ought not to see, it would just as surely prevent me from seeing what I ought to see. If the cutting off of my tongue would keep me from saying the unkind word, it would also keep me from saying that which was kind and helpful. The religion of surgery, therefore, could do nothing better than bring a purely negative gain. Since this is the case, it could not bring any gain at all. For no amount of "don'ts" can ever make a worthful man.

Add a column of ciphers as high as from here to Mars, and you still have absolutely nothing. Maim yourself, therefore, till you are as harmless as a corpse, and you will be just as useless as you are harmless.

3. We are sure, last of all, that Jesus did not suggest surgery as a remedy, because this would be contrary to all that he teaches elsewhere. A complete cure for sin is offered in himself. "They shall call his name Jesus, for he shall save his people from their sins." That means that he will save them at once from the penalty of sin and from the power of sin. "He was wounded for our transgressions; he was bruised for our iniquities. The chastisement of our peace was upon him, and with his stripes we are healed." There is a full and complete cure for sin in Jesus Christ if we are willing to accept it. He is our sufficiency, and there is none other. "For there is none other name under heaven given among men whereby we must be saved."

What, then, does Jesus mean by these strange words? He is seeking to bring home to our hearts a sense of the awfulness of sin. Sin causes the disorganization of our whole moral nature. It brings about sickness of soul. The words "holiness" and "health" come from the same Anglo-Saxon root. It would be as correct to speak of a holy body and a healthy soul as it is to speak of a healthy body and a holy soul. Lack of holiness means the lack of spiritual health. And how many of us are suffering from spiritual sickness! How many in the Church are confirmed spiritual invalids! And some of these are even on the official board. They are so sick that they are seldom found in the Sunday services. They are so sick that they are never found at the prayer meeting. They are so sick that they are seldom seen even at the business meetings of the Church. They are confirmed invalids, poor souls! The only place in the Church that they fill worthily is the hospital ward.

Then there are those who, while not positive invalids, have their spiritual health seriously impaired. They are still able to sit up. They are even able to come out at times on Sunday morning if the day is warm and bright with sunshine. But they are exceedingly delicate. They are very easily tired. A sermon five minutes too long tears their nerves to pieces. The effort required to get their hands into their pocketbooks makes them sleepless for half the following week. They try to work after a fashion. But they go about their religious duties with leaden feet. There is no sparkle in their eyes and no elasticity in their step. They are enjoying very wretched spiritual health.

Now, this spiritual sickness is the worst possible. This is true both as regards ourselves and others. There are many whose bodies are racked with pain who in their hearts rejoice with a joy unspeakable and full of glory. Sick in body, they are yet strong and vigorous in soul. Not only have they joy for themselves, but they are a means of blessing to others. Some of the most helpful people in the

DRASTIC OPERATIONS

world are the knights of the sick room, the heroes of the bed of pain.

Not long ago a certain preacher in the course of his pastoral duties went to see two women in very different circumstances. One of them was a little seamstress who had been left with a large family of younger brothers and sisters on her hands. She had poured her life into the task of rearing and educating them. And now she was dying of tuberculosis. But when the preacher spoke to her to encourage her, she smiled into his face and said: "O, I have rest and peace, peace and rest." While her body was slowly wasting away, her soul was enjoying the vigorous life of a spiritual athlete. The other woman was a great actress. She decked her couch with a nation's praise. The preacher congratulated her on her success. But she answered in a voice dull with weariness and disgust: "O, I am sick of it all! What I want is rest and peace, peace and rest." What she needed was to learn the secret of the little seamstress.

Not only does sin mean sickness, but it is a kind of sickness that will prove fatal unless it is thoroughly cured. For sin is like a cancer in that it is constantly spreading. If you have been persisting in some certain sin for the last ten years, that sin has a far greater hold on you now than it had at the beginning. And unless you get rid of it, it is going to mean the ruin of you. For the sickness of sin is a deadly sickness. There is nothing more sure than this: "The soul that sinneth, it shall die." Sin in the beginning may seem even to bring you a larger freedom and a larger life, but "sin, when it is finished, bringeth forth death." "For the wages of sin is death."

Sin, therefore, the Master tells us, is a thing so weakening, so deadening and damning that no price is too great to pay to be rid of it. No price is too great for Jesus Christ himself to pay, and no price is too great to be paid by you and me. Any sacrifice is to be counted as a mere trifle if it helps us toward being delivered from the terrible power of sin. According to our thinking, there are many calamities, there are many tragedies. But, according to Jesus, there is only one calamity, there is only one supreme tragedy, and that is the tragedy of sin, the tragedy of the quarrel of the soul with God. Sin must be given up even though the surrender seem more costly than the plucking out of the eye or the cutting off of the hand.

III

If our Lord does not propose to resort to surgery, how, then, does he propose to bring health to our souls? I think we might say for answer that he does it somewhat in the same way as the most skilled physician would go about restoring health to a diseased patient. There are times we recognize when an operation is necessary. In that case the patient is asked to trust his doctor. The faith expected of him is by no means a mean and meager faith. It is one great enough to make him willing

DRASTIC OPERATIONS

to lie down upon the operating table and be as completely in the power of his doctor as the clay is in the hands of the potter.

Such a faith many of us have exercised. Such a faith I have exercised. And this I have done with the consciousness that the cure the physician was going to work was not going to be an altogether full and adequate cure. For instance, when I had appendicitis I did not expect him to give me a sound appendix for one that was diseased. My highest hope was that he leave me with none at all. Such a cure you will recognize is, in the nature of things, negative. A complete cure would be the substitution of a healthful organ for one that was diseased.

But the greatest cures are those wrought without the use of the knife. It is that surgery that is performed naturally by a strong, healthy body. There was a time when the physician gave most of his attention to the killing of the disease. Now he gives the greater part of his attention to the building up of the body. If he can build up a strong body, then that strong body will kill the disease by itself.

In some kindred way does Christ cure. He invites us to put ourselves completely into his hands. This we should do with perfect confidence; for he never enters our lives to maim us. He never enters to subtract. He does not propose to rob us of one single one of our members or to impair one single faculty of mind or of heart. He comes, rather, to bring these to the fullness of their powers. He comes to bring them to their highest usefulness.

The hand that has been used for wrongdoing he does not propose to cut off, but to put to right uses. The eye that has been trained to see the unclean, he does not propose to smite with blindness. He rather enables it to see those things that it ought to see.

Our failure to appreciate this fact, I think, accounts for the weakness and the faultiness of so many of our lives. Much of our Christianity is little better than Pharisaism. We concern ourselves altogether too much with the negative side of life. Of course we do not attach too much importance to refusing to do the wrong. But we certainly attach altogether too little to the positive and aggressive doing of the right. Such a program is doomed to certain failure. You cannot slay your sins one at a time. You cannot pull up the noxious weeds in the garden of your soul one by one. The only remedy is to put yourself in the hands of Christ and let him plant your garden so full of flowers that there will not be room for the weeds. Your only chance to keep from doing the positive wrong is to be so busy doing the positive right that there is no inclination for anything else.

The little schoolhouse that I attended years ago was surrounded by a great grove of scrubby black oak. These trees had a wonderful way of clinging to their leaves. When the frost killed other leaves and cut them from the boughs of the trees, these oak leaves still clung, though they were as sear as any that lay on the ground. Then came the sharp winds of winter, but even they were powerless to break the hold of these dead leaves. Still later came the snow and the sleet and the ice, but their efforts were equally futile. But one day a wonderful surgeon clipped off all those leaves of death. Who was that surgeon? His name was Spring. Springtime got into the heart of those oaks, and the sap rose up, and new leaves pushed out and said to the old dead leaves: "This is my place." And thus Christ will save us. Therefore, "This I say, Walk in the Spirit, and you shall not fulfill the lust of the flesh."

XIII

THE MOTIVE TEST

Matthew 6: 1-18

"Take heed that ye do not your alms before men, to be seen of them: otherwise ye have no reward of your Father which is in heaven."

THE text is a word of warning. Jesus is pointing out a real danger. He is telling us of a foe that is lurking in our path. "Take heed," he says with emphatic earnestness. And since he is no nervous alarmist, since he never warns of perils that are imaginary, we should do well to listen reverently and attentively that we may avoid the danger of which he speaks.

I

What is the danger of which Jesus is giving us warning?

It is not idleness. Of course idleness is deadly. But out Lord assumes here that every one who is making any serious effort to be his follower will be a worker. He takes our good deeds for granted. He seems to count it as flatly impossible that we should claim to be disciples of his and yet pamper ourselves by living idle and useless lives. He regarded it as unthinkable that we should enter his service and yet

(166)

THE MOTIVE TEST

through cowardice or sheer laziness avoid all contact with the cross.

"Take heed that you do not your good deeds." That we are going to do good is assumed, you see, as a certainty. He recognizes, and expects us to do the same, that vital Christianity is impossible without sacrificial service. He told the story of a man who lost both himself and his talent, not because he had grossly misused his talent, but because he had not used it at all. He tells of a heart cleansed of evil that became sevenfold worse than it had ever been before, not because of any violent rush into sin, but because of sheer emptiness. Even a fig tree that bore nothing but leaves was blasted. It is, therefore, taken for granted that every Christian will be a worker. Idleness is a deadly evil, but it is not the object of the warning of Jesus here.

Nor is he warning, as might appear to some, against open and aggressive discipleship. When he urges secret prayer, he does not for that reason condemn public prayer. When he urges giving in so hidden and quiet a fashion that the left hand shall not know what the right hand is doing, he does not hereby condemn giving that is done in the eyes of the world. Our Lord never sets his sanction upon secret discipleship. He rather commands us to let our light so shine before men that they may see our good works and glorify our Father who is in heaven.

There are in every community certain very decent and respectable people who do good in a quiet way and yet who never openly identify themselves with

Christ and his Church. These are often held up as being better than the average Church member. And their virtues are further emphasized by the fact that they make no profession. But in their failure to do so they are hurting both themselves and others. For it is not a question of how good or useful they are without the Church; it is a question of how much better they might be and do if they would only acknowledge the One who is the source of whatever of real goodness there is in them. Now, our Lord is not smiling upon this rather pleasing type of paganism that through cowardice or mistaken modesty refuses to take an open stand for righteousness.

Against what, then, is he warning? The answer is in the text. "Take heed that ye do not your alms before men, to be seen of them." He is warning against a wrong motive. He is warning against that subtle temptation that comes to all of us who are trying to follow him, of looking to men for their approval rather than keeping our eyes and our hearts fixed on him. He recognizes the fact that the moral quality of a deed is determined by the motive that gives it birth; that, therefore, not only the evil, but the very good we do, may have no merit at all. The best of deeds may be poisoned and vitiated by a bad motive.

II

Jesus then proceeds to bring the motive test to bear upon the whole realm of our religious activities.

THE MOTIVE TEST 169

He brings it to bear on those obligations that look especially toward ourselves and that are summed up in fasting. Next, upon these obligations that look toward our brother and that are summed up in giving. Finally, he brings this test to bear on the obligations that look especially toward God and which are summed up in praying Let us look at them for a moment in the order in which they are here named.

1. Fasting is by no means prominent in the religious life of to-day. It has, however, the sanction of the greatest of the saints. It was certainly practiced by the early Christians. Paul made use of it. It was one of the weapons that he used to buffet his body and bring it under subjection. It was prominent at one time in our Church. Its purpose was the subduing of self. It was to make more complete the mastery of the spirit over the body. And I am not at all sure that we have not lost in so nearly casting aside what other saints have found helpful.

But fasting in the days of Jesus had come to have little religious value. So often those who were fasting were too eager to advertise the fact. Having decided to fast, they looked as mournful and woebegone as possible. They wanted all whom they met to read wretchedness in every line of their faces. The fact that they looked like incarnate pain was their way of proclaiming that they were subduing the physical, that they were very religious, and, therefore, entitled to the applause of men. They had their reward, said Jesus. They had it in the region in which they sought it—that is, the approval and recognition of their fellows. They looked to men for their reward and received in some measure that for which they looked.

2. "When you give," said Jesus, "or when you serve in any way, do not sound a trumpet before you as the hypocrites do in the synagogue." Our Lord does not mean that these gentlemen actually blew a blast when they gave a gift. He does mean that they gave for display, that they were ostentatious in their giving. They gave with their eyes fixed on the faces of men. Whatever they did, they did, not for the divine approval, but for the praise and applause they might win from their fellows. Thus giving and serving, their reward was of the earth earthy.

3. "When you pray," said Jesus, "do not pray to men, pray to God." To make this possible Jesus urges that we enter into the closet and shut the door. This we are to do that we may shut ourselves in with him. This we are to do that we may become the more conscious of the Divine Presence. This does not, of course, require a literal closet. We may thus retire even in the presence of the crowd. But those who have mastered this secret of being alone with God amidst the crowd have usually learned it in the hush and quiet of their own closets. They have also usually been at no small pains to learn it, for it is not easy to pray to God rather than to men. It is extremely difficult for many of us in the offering of our public prayers. The consciousness of the presence of men so often crowds out the consciousness of

THE MOTIVE TEST

God. We find ourselves praying a prayer perhaps quite as eloquent as that famous one that was declared to be the most eloquent ever addressed to a Boston audience, but also quite as futile. Such a prayer is heard only by the same kind of ears that heard the one in Boston, and brings no higher reward.

Then, our Lord gives further directions for praying, that while not concerned with motive, yet are exceedingly pertinent and greatly in need of emphasis. He warns against vain repetition, that fatal fluency in prayer that leads to the pouring out a mere deluge of words. Prayer, he tells us, is not judged by its quantity, but by its quality. It is easy to say endless words if we want nothing, but when the load is heavy and the sword has really pierced through our hearts, we come to the point very quickly and cry out with Peter: "Lord, save me."

Then, we are not to pray for the sake of informing God. I heard a prayer not long since that reminded me of *Pathe's Weekly*. The brother seemed trying to give the Lord a résumé of the world's history up to the present time. "Remember," says Jesus, "your Father knows what you have need of." You are not praying to inform him. You are praying to give him a chance to meet your needs. Prayer is a means of opening the door to the Christ, who, with all-sufficient grace, is already knocking and who will enter the moment you fling open the door.

III

What is the danger of thus giving away to wrong motives?

1. It poisons the very fount of life. It marks us as wrong at the heart and center of our being.

2. Since the fountain is wrong, the stream that flows out from it must of necessity also be wrong. Remember that the motive determines the moral quality of the deed. No service can be really good that is done from a base and sordid motive. We realize this in our dealings one with another. We appreciate only that which is done for Love's sake and not for the selfish interest of the one who serves us.

This is true regardless of how seemingly beautiful the deed may be. What a beautiful something was the kiss of Judas if one did not know the motive that lay back of it! Suppose Judas had been loyal and sincere. Suppose he had truly said in his heart: "My Master is in danger. They are going to arrest him. Possibly they will put him to death. His friends may forsake him. But whatever others may do, I, for one, am going to stand by him, and in token of my loyalty and love I give him this kiss." If the kiss of Judas had been sincere, his story would have been one of the sweetest ever told. But the fact that he took the most beautiful caress of love to make it an instrument of treachery has made his story about the blackest ever told.

No deed done from a wrong motive has any merit,

THE MOTIVE TEST

even though it may be greatly useful. In truth, many thoroughly selfish deeds are useful. Many a prayer has been blessed to the edification of some saint when it had no merit at all for him that offered it. Many a gift has been highly useful that was given sordidly and selfishly. Many a sermon has been used to the salvation of souls when the preacher had absolutely nothing to his credit in the eyes of Him "who sees things clearly and sees them whole." I doubt if anything better could have happened to Joseph than to have been sold into slavery. He was gifted. He was a dreamer of great dreams. But he was a spoiled son of a doting father. He was a bit of a self-centered prig. His trying education in the hard school through which he passed made a man of him. It made it possible for him to pass from a nomad's tent to a palace on the Nile without having his head turned. It made it possible for him to save countless lives. But for all that, no credit was due to his selfish and cruel brothers. Joseph recognized that. "Ye meant it unto me for evil, but God meant it unto good." Through the grace of God, what was intended for a curse became a blessing. But no credit was due to those who intended it to be a curse.

3. A wrong motive makes impossible any God-given reward. No reward is given, because none is deserved. There are those who have run past the morality of the New Testament and object to any offer of reward at all. But Jesus did not hesitate to speak again and again of rewards. He implies here,

and the New Testament implies emphatically elsewhere, that there is a reward for those who serve for love's sake. There is the reward of a growing likeness to Christ. There is also the reward of usefulness. Then there is the reward of the Saviour's "Well done." But the selfish servant can have no reward of our Father who is in heaven.

IV

How are we to take heed? How are we to rid ourselves of these wrong motives that so tend to vitiate even the best and noblest of our deeds? We are not going to do so by continually questioning our motives. We are not going to do so by constantly keeping our fingers upon our spiritual pulse. We are not going to do so by persistently looking at our tongues and morbidly subjecting ourselves to examination. It is possible to push self-scrutiny too far. I think I have known more than one to become physical invalids by keeping too close tab on themselves. And it is altogether possible for us to become spiritual invalids in the same way.

But, having said that, I must add that it is well now and then to face the facts about ourselves. How about our motives? Suppose we make this test. It is one that a wise man has suggested. Do we give over our good deeds when men fail to applaud? Do we work so long as we are chairman of the committee and quit when another takes our place? Do we attend church so long as we are greeted warmly and folks seem glad to see us, and

THE MOTIVE TEST

do we quit if they pass us by for a service or two? If such is the case, we had better beware. Our eyes are likely to be upon men more than upon God.

But, having faced the evil, what is its cure? Here, as often elsewhere, this sermon demands a gospel that will regenerate. How do we drive out the darkness? We cannot do so with a club. The darkness goes when the light comes in. How are we to get rid of our wrong motives? We cannot pull them up by the roots and throw them away one at a time. We can only destroy them by bringing in of right motives. And right motives come when Jesus Christ comes. "Without me," he tells us frankly, "you can do nothing." "You need not be surprised that you fail, not only in service, but even in the motives for service, if you attempt to go it alone. I am the one absolute essential. You must have me; for, if you have me, you have love."

And love is enough. For, just as no deed, however seemingly great, is of any merit without love, so the very least is of abiding merit if love is its motive. "Though I bestow all my goods to feed the poor, and though I give my body to be burned, and have not love, it profiteth me nothing. But if I give even so much as a cup of cold water for love's sake, I am forever enriched. For it is love that God wants. He says: "Son, give me thine heart." And we are kinsfolk with God. It is love that the human heart wants. Love is the cure for every evil. It is the fulfilling of the law. Everything without love leaves us paupers. If we have love and nothing else, we are unspeakably rich.

> "If all the ships I have at sea
> Should come a-sailing home to me,
> Weighed down with gems and wealth untold,
> With glory, honor, riches, gold,
> Ah, well! the harbor would not hold
> So many ships as there would be,
> If all my ships should come to me.
>
> If half the ships I have at sea
> Should come a-sailing home to me,
> Ah, well! I should have the wealth as great
> As any king that sits in state,
> So rich the treasures there would be
> In half the ships I have at sea.
>
> If just one ship I have at sea
> Should come a-sailing home to me,
> Ah, well! the storm clouds then might frown,
> For if the others all went down,
> Still rich and proud and glad I'd be
> If that one ship came home to me.
>
> If that one ship were lost at sea,
> And all the others came to me,
> Weighed down with gems and silks untold,
> With glory, honor, riches, gold,
> The poorest soul on earth I'd be
> If that one ship came not to me.
>
> Ah, skies be clear! Ah, winds be free!
> Bring all my ships safe home to me.
> But if thou sendest some a-wrack,
> To nevermore come sailing back,
> Send any, all, that skim the sea,
> But bring my love ship home to me."

That is the cry of the human heart. That is the cry also of the heart of our Lord. Therefore, "Take heed that ye do not your alms before men, to be seen of them: otherwise ye have no reward of your Father which is in heaven."

XIV

A WISE INVESTMENT

Matthew 6: 19, 20

> "Lay not up for yourselves treasures upon earth, where moth and rust doth corrupt, and where thieves break through and steal: but lay up for yourselves treasures in heaven, where neither moth nor rust doth corrupt, and where thieves do not break through and steal."

I

The text deals with a matter of vital importance to every one of us. Jesus is instructing us as to where to invest. He is telling us where to desposit our treasure. "Treasure," you answer sadly, or, maybe resentfully; "I have no treasure. I am having the hardest kind of fight to keep the wolf from the door. I am having to skimp and save and cut corners constantly to make ends meet. I cannot deposit a penny anywhere. Preach to the money magnates. Preach to the misers. I hear that two hundred and ten men control two-thirds of the wealth of the whole world. Preach to them, if you have anything to say about treasure, but do not waste your time and my own as well by talking to me about where to lay up my treasure, because I have none."

But in saying this you are altogether mistaken. Everybody is the possessor of some kind of treasure.

A WISE INVESTMENT

Of course it does not always consist of silver and gold. It may not consist of stocks and bonds, of houses and lands. Our treasure is that something that we love the best. It is that which we most yearn to possess, if it is not ours. It is that which we most fear to lose, if we already possess it. It is that something to which our affections, our wills, our whole being clings. Your treasure may be entirely different from mine. And mine may be entirely different from that of my neighbor. But every man has a treasure, and every man is investing his treasure somewhere.

II

Now, not only are we all investing our treasure, but we are putting it into one of two places. We are either laying up treasure upon the earth, or we are laying it up in heaven. Our choice is strictly limited to these two places. There is no third place where we may invest.

What is it to lay up treasure upon the earth? It is to put the world first in our thoughts, our plans, our affections. Jesus gives us a striking example of what it means to invest our all in this world in the story of the unjust steward. This man received notice that he is soon to lose his position. What is his reaction? He does not consider first how he is to hold fast his integrity. His first and supreme consideration is how he is to have bread to eat and a roof over his head, after he has been retired, without the pains of working or the shame of begging. "I cannot dig, and to beg I am ashamed." To gain this end he plays the rascal and induces his lord's creditors to play the rascal with him. Now, he may have cared for honesty and truth and uprightness, but, if he did, these were certainly secondary. His supreme care was for things. He was a man whose treasure was deposited in the bank of this world.

To lay up treasure in heaven is to take the opposite course. The first step in this direction is to accept Jesus Christ as our Lord and Master. It is to seek first the kingdom of God and his righteousness. Whoever enthrones Christ in his life lays up treasure in heaven. Jesus makes this fact clear in his dealings with the rich young ruler. This young man, spurred by a conscious lack, came and kneeled before the Master. "What lack I?" is his question. "You have made a wrong investment," our Lord seems to answer. "Go sell whatsoever thou hast, and give to the poor, and thou shalt have treasure in heaven: and come, take up thy cross, and follow me." The first and supreme essential, therefore, in the laying up of our treasure in heaven is to make a personal choice of Jesus Christ as our Saviour and Lord.

Then, having made this personal choice, we lay up treasure in heaven by living in loving and loyal obedience to Christ. For long centuries men sought how they might turn baser metals into gold, but they sought in vain. Through Jesus Christ we learn a far more priceless secret. We learn how to transmute the commonplace services that we may render in our everyday lives into wealth that will outlast the ages. Every deed that we do for love's sake becomes an eternal investment. Even one who renders so small a service as the giving of a cup of cold water in His name will be drawing dividends when this world of ours has become a wreck.

Is not this clearly taught in the parable to which we referred a moment ago? The first aim of this steward was to provide for his material welfare. This he did by making a shrewd use of his master's goods. And Jesus urges a like wisdom upon us who claim to be the children of light. He urges that we so use our possessions, our wealth, our talents, our opportunities to serve, that we may provide for our eternal future. "Make to yourselves friends of the mammon of unrighteousness; that, when ye fail, they may receive you into everlasting habitations." That is, we are to so love and give and serve here as to lay up for ourselves treasures in heaven.

Not only are we laying up treasure upon the earth or in heaven, but we are doing so exclusively. That is, we are putting all our treasure in heaven, or we are putting all our treasure upon the earth. Wise business men like to scatter their investments. They fear to venture their all in one single enterprise. If their investments are scattered, a loss may be compensated by a gain. If, on the other hand, all is invested in one place, then a loss means bankruptcy. Just so there are those who seek to scatter their investments by undertaking to lay up treasure both in earth and heaven. But this, Jesus tells us emphatically, is utterly impossible. Look at the Pharisees, for example. They were a serious-minded and zealous people. They fasted, they prayed, they gave. They were at pains in the performance of their religious duties. Nor are we to assume for a moment that they had absolutely no care for the Divine approval. They desired to please God in all that they did. But their supreme desire was to please men. They received their reward, Jesus tells us. Men did approve, but God did not. Therefore all their treasure went to one place, and that place was the world.

This does not mean, of course, that men cannot act from mixed motives. They can and very often do. But there is always one motive that is supreme. "No man can serve two masters: for either he will hate the one and love the other; or else he will hold to the one and despise the other. Ye cannot serve God and mammon." When we come to the last rub, when we are pushed into the final corner, it is either love of the material or love of the spiritual that dominates us. We either put self first or we put Christ first. To put the world first is to shut out the love of God. That is what John meant when he said: "Love not the world, neither the things that are in the world. If any man love the world, the love of the Father is not in him."

III

Now since we are all investors, and since every man must invest in one of two places, it becomes us

A WISE INVESTMENT

to examine wisely and well these two opportunities that are offered. If we make a foolish financial investment, we may recover. Many a man has lost a fortune only to make a larger. But if we go wrong in this vital matter of which our Lord is speaking, there is no promise of a second chance. The loss is an eternal loss. "For what shall it profit a man, if he shall gain the whole world, and lose his own soul? Or what shall a man give in exchange for his soul?"

1. Look, first, at the opportunities offered by the world. This present world certainly has something to say for itself. There is the appeal of the multitude, for instance. "Commit your treasure to me," says the world, "and you will find yourself a part of a great crowd. My clients are many. My banking house is thronged by a vast multitude of eager and enthusiastic investors. Some of them are noted for their business sagacity. They are famous for their shrewdness and foresight. Some of them have grown so powerful that they fairly make the windows of Wall Street and Lombard Street to tremble whenever they pass by. Many of them declare boastingly: 'Everything I touch turns to gold.' My patrons are indeed an impressive multitude."

Then the world has this further appeal. It speaks ro the man who prides himself on the fact that he is practical. It says to such a one: "Treasure in heaven may be good enough for one who is very old, or for one upon whose brow the death dews are gathering. But when one is well and strong it seems little better than 'such stuff as dreams are made on.'

As a practical man, therefore, you want something more substantial. You want something that you can see, something that you can hold in your hand, can put into your pocket, or deposit in a safety vault. You are too shrewd by far to be satisfied by an unseen wealth. You have the good sense to 'take the cash and let the credit go.' I know there was once an old man who was foolish enough to say, 'The things that are seen are temporal, but the things that are not seen are eternal.' But according to his own testimony he had suffered the loss of all things, and died at last without even a cloak to keep him warm. He had nothing, in fact, except abiding peace, the handclasp of Christ, and the hope of eternity."

But since I am to invest and since I cannot afford to lose my treasure, I feel that I must ask one or two questions. The first is a question that cannot fail to occur at once to every intelligent investor. "World, suppose I invest with you, can you guarantee me against loss? You see I invested in a company once that went broke. Therefore, I am a bit timid. I must be sure. I acknowledge that your investors are numerous. I confess that many of them seem very wise and very prudent. But I am still not absolutely sure that the investment you offer is safe. Now, if I deposit with you, can you say with confidence, with absolute certainty, in fact, that my investment will be forever safe? Can I count on it? or is there a dark possibility that, in spite of all your parading of prominent names, I might lose all that I possess?"

What answer does the world give? What answer can it give? Only one. This is the answer: "If you deposit with me, I cannot say with positive assurance that your investment will be forever safe. But I can say with absolute certainty that you will be perfectly sure to lose it. Nothing under heaven can possibly be more sure than that." And to that fact, every one, regardless of where he invests, must agree. Every penny, every ounce of treasure, that we invest in this world we are absolutely sure to lose.

This is true regardless of the nature of our treasure. If it is in money, we shall lose that. When, I do not know. It may be to-day, it may be to-morrow, but certainly we shall lose it some time. How we shall lose, I cannot say. The possibilities for such disaster are numerous. If we lose by no other process, then Highwayman Death will at last wrench it from our fingers and fling us empty-handed and poverty-stricken out into the night. Very often the loss comes before death. A few years ago a man was carrying water in a certain city for ten cents per hour. Yet, that man owned a mausoleum that cost him two hundred thousand dollars. He had builded it in the days of his prosperity, but reverses had come. Now he had nothing left but a resting place for his dead body.

Then we just as inevitably lose our higher forms of worldly wealth. Your treasure may be physical beauty. You may be as fair as an artist's dream. But one thing is sure, you will not always be so. The thieving years will rob you of your charm. You may have an intellect that flashes like a meteor. But one day your brilliant brain will cease to function. Dean Swift sat looking at a book that he had written in the heyday of his power. "My God," he said, "what a genius I had when I wrote that book!" He was speaking truth. He was surely one of the most brilliant writers of prose that ever set pen to paper. But he was confessing the fact that he was not a genius any more. Of all certainties, therefore, nothing is more certain than this, if our treasure is invested in this world we are one day going to lose it.

Then there is a second question I ask this world: "You have been honest with me thus far. You tell me that though my deposit may be safe with you for a while, I am sure to lose it in the end. What about the peace and the joy it will give me while it lasts? I would like a few moments of solid satisfaction even if they are brief. If I invest with you, can you guarantee to me such satisfaction before the final crash comes?" "I cannot," is the answer. "What you deposit with me is sure to be lost in the end, and it will fail absolutely to bring you abiding peace while you possess it.

To the truth of that statement every man whose treasure is in this present world must agree. It is no matter of wonder that the man of the world is full of care. He is so open to attack. He is capable of

A WISE INVESTMENT

being wounded at so many points. The disaster that must come some day, may come any day.

"In sooth, I know not why I am so sad,"

says Antonio in the "Merchant of Venice." But it is easy for his companions to guess the reason.

"Your mind is tossing on the ocean,"

his friend tells him.

"Believe me, sir, had I such venture forth,
. . . . . . I should be still
Plucking the grass, to know where sits the wind;
. . . . . . My wind, cooling my broth
Would blow me to an ague, when I thought
What harm a wind too great might do at sea."

These, then, are the facts we are to face: However great the claims of the world, it can offer nothing better than certain loss in the end and restlessness and worry while we possess.

2. Let us look next at our other opportunity. We may lay up treasure in heaven. This is what Jesus is urging us to do. "Lay up for yourselves treasure in heaven." Is his admonition sound? Has he solid reason for giving such command? Suppose we put to him the same questions that we put to the world. Can he give a satisfactory answer? Jesus leaves us in no doubt in this matter. Where the world fails he claims to be entirely adequate.

First, if we deposit with him we have a positive guarantee against all possibility of loss. The treasure that we lay up in heaven is surely safe forevermore. Moths cannot devour it, rust cannot corrupt it, thieves cannot wrench it from our hands. This is true because to lay up treasure in heaven is to have wealth not only in that house not made with hands, it is to have wealth within our own hearts in the life that now is. To make Christ our banker is to be rich in faith and hope and love in the here and now. It is to be rich in that most worthful of all treasure, Christlike character. Such wealth the world is powerless to give and is equally powerless to take away.

Years ago there lived near my old home a man who was a thorough-going miser. He worked hard and spent little and gave nothing. In this manner he managed to accumulate some five thousand dollars in gold. He would not deposit this money in a bank. He hid it in a secret place known only to himself. But one night a highwayman paid him a visit. He stuck the muzzle of an angry-looking gun close up against the man's face and asked him for a donation. The miser consented. He gave him every dollar, though it broke his heart. "Why did you not argue the question with him?" an old friend asked the next day. "Why did you not refuse?" "Hell was too close," was the simple answer. All this man's treasure was on the outside of him. None was in his heart.

But I read this story of another man, a college professor. He was rather a frail chap physically, but he had a clear mind and a clean heart. He was in love with a girl of great vigor and charm. He had a rival who was an athletic fellow, magnetic and at-

A WISE INVESTMENT

tractive. This rival seemed to have everything that could appeal. Therefore, nobody was surprised when he became engaged to the girl of their choice. But he was lacking in character. In his eagerness for easy money, he stole certain trust funds that were committed to his care. The circumstances were such that it became the duty of the professor to witness against him. And it was through this testimony that he was convicted and sent to serve a term in the penitentiary.

One dark night years later, when the rain was falling in torrents, the professor was alone in his library. Suddenly he felt a breath of cold wind. He looked up from his work, and there before him stood his rival in the garb of a convict with a revolver in his hand. "I have dreamed of this meeting for a long time," said the intruder bitterly. "You have ruined my life and now I am going to make you pay." "I did not ruin your life," the little professor answered quietly. "You ruined it yourself when you became a thief. Nobody can ruin one's live but one's self." "How I have suffered," the convict continued. "And how I have longed to make you suffer as I have suffered!" "But that you cannot do," the professor replied. "You can kill me, of course, but you are entirely powerless to make me suffer as you have suffered. If you kill me, my suffering will be physical only, and doubtless very brief. Death will be for me the gateway into a fuller life. Therefore, you cannot make me suffer as you have suffered." This man possessed a wealth that thieves cannot break through and steal. No wonder the convict stood awed in his presence. His foe had that which is proof against any weapon that man can wield.

Not only is the investment that we make with Jesus safe, not only will it meet our needs through all eternity, but it will satisfy us in the here and now. "Godliness is profitable unto all things, having promise of the life that now is, and of that which is to come." If we lay up our treasure in heaven, it is our privilege to live the care-free life. Worry ought to be an utter impossibility for one who has made God his banker. This is certainly the conviction of Jesus. Three times over he says, "Be not anxious." We are not to worry about things. We are not to worry about to-morrow. He who keeps our treasure safe to-day will keep it safe forever. "I know whom I have believed, and am persuaded that he is able to keep that which I have committed unto him against that day." Therefore,

"Build a fence of trust around each day and therein stay;
 Look not through the sheltering bars upon to-morrow,
 For God will help thee bear whate'er there is of joy or sorrow."

XV

"ASK—SEEK—KNOCK"

Matthew 7: 7, 8

"Ask, and it shall be given you; seek, and ye shall find; knock, and it shall be opened unto you: for every one that asketh receiveth; and he that seeketh findeth; and to him that knocketh it shall be opened."

WHAT a tremendous declaration! What a staggering promise! Jesus was a continuous source of amazement to those who companied with him. He was the most thrilling personality that this world has ever seen. Over and over again we are told that they were astonished at him. He was constantly making men gasp. He was persistently filling them with boundless amazement. Those who knew him best had their otherwise ordinary and commonplace days changed by him into days of winsome and unbelievable surprises. But, judging by the record, there was nothing that Jesus did that so stirred the wonder and longing of his disciples as what he taught, expecially by example, about prayer.

Of course they were constantly amazed at him as a wonder worker. But never once, so far as we know, did they come to him and say wistfully: "Lord, teach us to work wonders." They marveled at his preaching. How fascinating he was! How he put his hands on the commonplace things that lay all about, salt and light, bread and water, and set them to uttering "thoughts that breathe and words that burn." Yet they never asked him to teach them to preach. But one day they came upon him at his prayers. They were as garrulous as a bunch of schoolboys, perhaps. Maybe they were disputing as to who should be greatest. But suddenly they heard his voice in prayer. They got a view of his upturned face. A holy hush fell over them. A deep reverence filled their hearts. Here, they felt, was real prayer. Here was something vital. Here was One who was having first-hand dealings with God. And though they had been accustomed to hearing prayers all their lives, though they themselves had been men of prayer, they felt that they had never witnessed real prayer before. And when the Master had ended they came to him with wistful hearts and said: "Lord, teach us to pray."

What a privilege to be taught by one who knows. And Jesus is certainly the supreme expert in the high art of prayer. Never was there another who used this matchless instrument of peace and power so constantly and so well. He knows from his own experience the worth of prayer. He knows its possibilities. He speaks as one having authority. And this is what he has to say: "Ask, and it shall be given you; seek, and ye shall find; knock, and it shall be opened unto you: for every one that asketh receiveth; and he that seeketh findeth; and to him that knocketh it shall be opened." A stupendous promise, surely! One that is wonderful in its richness. But even then the wealth of it is little more amazing than the treatment that it receives at the hands of many professing Christians.

I

How do we who claim to be followers of Christ treat this promise? How do we treat the privilege and responsibility of prayer?

1. There are those who make practically nothing of prayer. They face a rich promise like this with listless and lack-luster eyes and leave it unappreciated and untouched. I do not think I am in any sense a pessimist. I am certain that I am not an unsympathetic critic of the Church of to-day. But I am driven to this conviction: the modern Church is not a praying Church. The vast majority of the membership of our various denominations make very little of prayer. They believe in it after a fashion. They believe that for certain saints of their acquaintance it may be of value; but as for themselves, they give it but little effort, little thought, and little time.

For instance, take ourselves. How much do we pray? "Enter into thy closet and shut the door, and pray to thy Father which is in secret, and thy Father which seeth in secret shall reward thee openly." Have you tried this out? Do you have a secret place of prayer? Is it the habit of your life to meet God alone each day? How about this morning? Did you pray before coming to church? Did you ask God to prepare you for the service? Did you pray his blessing on the teachers of the Sunday school? Did you pray that the minister might come into the pulpit in the fullness of the blessing of the gospel of Christ? We are decent, respectable people, who love the Church after a fashion, but most of us are not people of prayer.

2. Then there are those who have taken this promise more seriously, but have fumbled it. They have blundered in the use of it. Somehow, for them at least, it has failed to work. "Every one that asketh receiveth." "No, no," they say, "that is not true. I have asked, and I have not received. I have sought, at times desperately, and I have not found. I have knocked with bruised fists and broken heart, but the door has not been flung open to me." And the truth of this cannot be denied. There are those who do ask and fail to receive. There are those who seek, after a fashion, and do not find. Some of these become discouraged and indifferent. Others become rebellious and embittered. A woman of this type came into my office sometime ago. She looked at me with eyes red with weeping and said bitterly: "I prayed for my boy, God knows I did, but my prayer was not answered. God simply did nothing at all, and I will never pray again as long as I live."

3. Then there are others who have found that prayer really works. When I read this gracious promise, "Ask, and ye shall receive; seek, and ye shall find; knock, and it shall be opened," there were those who said a whole-hearted "amen." They have found prayer a source of comfort and power. They have found it a means of enrichment both to

themselves and to those for whom they have prayed. "I sought the Lord, and he heard me, and delivered me from all my fears." This Psalmist had found that God really does give good things to them that ask him. I do not know just what his fears were. He may have been afraid of the sins of his youth. He may have been afraid of the temptations of to-morrow. He may have been afraid of some deadly disease. He may have been afraid of loneliness or of the home-going of one dearer than life. But, whatever his fears, as he prayed, they vanished, and he found himself enjoying the security of the Everlasting Arms. So multitudes have claimed something of the measureless wealth offered by this promise.

II

How did they succeed? How may we?

1. We must ask. Now, asking carries certain implications that we cannot neglect.

(1) To ask implies a sense of need. No one ever really prays without a felt need. The Pharisee can strike a pose in the eyes of men. He can compliment himself, he can criticize his brother, he can congratulate the Lord on having such a paragon of a servant as himself. But he cannot pray. There is another man present who has nothing to his credit. He is not half so decent as the Pharisee. He is an outcast, a publican. But he does all the praying that is done on that occasion. This is the case because, staggering under a load of guilt that he feels he cannot carry, he cries out of the depths of a

great need: "God be merciful unto me, a sinner." And the asking that has reality in it is always born of a sense of need.

(2) To ask is to apply to a person. Therefore the asking of the text implies contact with a Personality. It implies contact with the supreme Personality, even God himself. But such contact can be made only by one who has a faith that leads to obedience. Our Lord is infinitely approachable. To the most stained and hopeless he gives a welcome. But there is one for whom prayer is impossible. That is the one who will not surrender. Did you ever try to pray when you knew you were clinging to something that was hateful to God? Did you ever try to pray when you were determined on a course of action that you knew was contrary to the will of God? If you have, then you know what I mean. Praying under such circumstances is an utter impossibility. You cannot make contact, you cannot ask God. You may ask space, you may ask the black shadows that encircle you, but you cannot make contact with God. "If I regard iniquity in my heart, the Lord will not hear me."

It is the unsurrendered will that accounts for many an unanswered prayer. When you take the business of praying seriously, when you seem on the point of winning your way into the secret place of the Most High, what is that something that intervenes and makes a vital approach impossible? When you are praying for your children, does the need of a family altar slip into your mind? Do you see that as your duty and privilege, and yet tell God that it is impossible? Does the face of a friend to whom you owe an apology intervene? Does a practice that is questionable and that you know you ought to give up blur your vision and make your petition seem a sheer futility? It need not be so. There is a way of victory. John found that way, and he gives this joyful testimony; "Whatsoever we ask, we receive of him, because we keep his commandments, and do those things that are pleasing in his sight."

(3) Then, the asking of which Jesus speaks is asking according to the will of God. There are numerous times, of course, when we know what the will of God is, when we have a definite promise to plead. When this is the case, we can pray unconditionally for an answer. But there are other times when the will of God is not known. In such cases we are to pray in submission to his will. Surely we do not desire that he do for us contrary to his own will, for that could not be best. "That is the confidence that we have in him, that, if we ask anything according to his will, he heareth us: and if we know that he hear us, whatsoever we ask, we know that we have the petitions that we desired of him." For our own sakes, God cannot answer our prayers when we ask for that which is contrary to his will. He has not promised to do so. He has promised the opposite.

But, in spite of this, we are prone to misunderstand. Some years ago it was my privilege to know two women who were exceptionally beautiful in their religious lives. They had a brother who was slowly weakening under the ravages of tuberculosis. They set themselves to pray for his recovery. They went to God with great confidence and determination and asked unconditionally that he restore that brother to health. They persuaded themselves that they had received the desired answer. Therefore, when the doctor said that the patient was dying, they would not believe it. They declared that it simply could not be true; that God would not fail them. But he died, nevertheless. And with his death, gloom settled down upon those two good women, and they came very near plunging into utter atheism.

But God had not failed them. They had simply misunderstood his promise. God knows what is best for us. He knows the end from the beginning. Therefore in his mercy he will not allow us to ruin ourselves by our sometimes foolish prayers. Jesus emphasizes the reasonableness of this by appealing to ourselves. "You, too," he says, "are accustomed to hear prayers and answer them according to your wisdom. If a son ask bread of any of you that is a father, will he give him a stone? Or if he ask a fish, will he give him a serpent? If ye then, being evil, know how to give good gifts unto your children, how much more shall your Father which is in heaven give good things to them which ask him?" It is not the willingness of God that is here emphasized; it is his wisdom in giving. We, in spite of our limitations, know, in some measure, how to answer the prayers of our children. How much more may we rely upon the wisdom of God in this matter?

Now, there are times when we who are parents answer prayers on the part of our children that are at once foolish and hurtful. Our wisdom cannot always be trusted. There are times, also, when we answer prayers, not because we think it wise to do so, but because it is the easiest way out. Many a father has wrecked his boy by answering his foolish prayers. If my boy were to ask me for something that I knew would do him nothing but harm, I should refuse him. And the more I loved him, the more emphatic would be my refusal. A prominent man in our city went a few weeks ago to bring his son home. That son had been shot in an underworld brawl. He had turned criminal. How did his own father account for the tragedy? In these words: "I gave him too much money and allowed him to have his own way." We often make this mistake. We often hurt our children by answering their foolish prayers. But God never does. He is perfect in wisdom as well as in love.

Because this is true, if you look back over your yesterdays you will find it in your heart to thank God, not only for prayers answered, but also for requests not granted. The mother of St. Augustine prayed with desperate earnestness that her son might not go to Italy. He was already dissolute and wayward. She felt that Italy would be the ruin of him. But to Italy he went in spite of all her prayers, and it was in Italy that he found Jesus Christ. Paul prayed with desperate confidence that God would remove his thorn. But God did not grant his request. He desired that his servant have the best. The removal of the thorn would have been only second best. Jesus asked in Gethsemane that the cup might pass from him. But God did not grant his request. Jesus did not desire him to grant it unless it was in accordance with his will. It was through this rejection of his prayer that Jesus "shall see of the travail of his soul and be satisfied."

2. Then, we must not only ask, we must seek. Seeking means asking plus effort. That is, there are times when we must help God in the answering of our prayers. We recognize the truth of this in the realm of the material. Jesus taught us to pray: "Give us this day our daily bread." But, having prayed that prayer, we do not betake ourselves to lives of idleness. My father was a farmer. He was also a man of prayer. But when he asked God to prosper his farming he did not sit down and leave the whole matter with him. He did not tell the Lord to sow wheat in one field and oats in another and plant corn in another. Had he done so, he would have starved. It is wise to pray for the blessings of God on our business. But our prayers go for nothing if we do not work.

The same is true in the realm of the spiritual. If I pray to God for spiritual health, in order for my prayers to be effective I must obey the laws of health. How foolish it would be for me to ask God to make me strong physically and then eat nothing at all! How foolish it would be to ask him for physical health and then gormandize upon food that I knew did not agree with me! Yet there are many of us praying for growth in grace, praying to be made more saintly, yet we are leaving off the food by which the soul grows. Or we do things every day that do not agree with us.

Take the amusement question, for instance. There are many decent and respectable folks who spend much time in the ballroom and more time at the card table. They do not seem to be greatly harmed by it. But how about you? Do these things agree with you? A young lady of rosy cheeks and vigorous health told me sometime ago that she drank nine cups of coffee a day. But one cup is too much for me. It is not a question of the effect of this or that practice on another, but how does it affect you? Does it hinder your growth in grace? If it hinders, give it up, or praying will come to nothing. It is useless to say, "Thy will be done," unless you set yourself resolutely to the task of doing the will of God as he gives you to see it.

The same holds true in our efforts to help others. We are taught to pray, "Thy kingdom come." But we must do more than pray for it. We must work for it. It is well to pray for our children, but we must do more. It is fine to pray for our Church, but we must do more. Sometime ago I heard one crying aloud in an almost empty church: "O Lord, go out into the highways and hedges and compel them to come in!" But that is just what the Lord told us to do. The sin of the priest and the Levite was not the fact that they did not pray for the man that was wounded by the wayside. In all probability they did so. The tragedy was that they did nothing else. We must coöperate with God in the answering of our prayers.

3. Finally, we must knock. Knocking is asking plus effort plus persistence. Jesus makes plain, in the story of the man who had a guest at midnight, what he means by knocking. This host, when he found that his larder was empty, went and knocked on the door of the house of his friend. At first his request was refused, but he persisted until the door was opened and the request was granted. Therefore do you go and do likewise is the teaching of Jesus. Ask, seek, knock. Persist in your asking and seeking until you get an answer.

It is necessary to persist because the answer to prayer is sometimes delayed. Of course this delay is often the fault of ourselves. At other times there is delay because our request is of such a nature that it cannot be answered at once. Christ prayed that his people might be one. That prayer has not been fully answered yet. But the answer is on the way. If, therefore, your prayer is not answered at once, do not give up. Jesus knows that you will be sorely tempted to do so. That is the reason he gave such marked emphasis to the necessity of persistence. "He spake a parable to this end, that men ought always to pray, and not to faint." It is so easy to give over the struggle. But to do so means that we lose the victory. We are to persist, not in order to make God hear us; we are to do so because God surely will hear us. Therefore, "if the vision tarry, wait for it." Do not faint; remember that "everyone that asketh receiveth; and he that seeketh findeth; and to him that knocketh it shall be opened."

XVI

THE WAY OF LIFE

Matthew 7: 13, 14

"Enter ye in at the strait gate: for wide is the gate, and broad is the way, that leadeth to destruction, and many there be which go in thereat: because strait is the gate, and narrow is the way, which leadeth unto life, and few there be that find it."

I

"Enter by the narrow gate." This text is at once a command and an invitation. It has a certain appeal to the high and the heroic within us. But it has also that which tends to shock and to repel. This is true, first, because here, again, the Master is dividing men into two classes, and we do not altogether like that. As he speaks he sees before him a vast multitude. In the bosom of the centuries he sees multitudes infinitely more vast. These multitudes are made up of all sorts and conditions of men. They belong to all kindreds and tribes and tongues. He sees the wise and the foolish, the cultured and the unlearned, the hopeful and the despondent, the young and the old, the rich and the poor. But as he looks upon this vast and mixed throng he sees them arrange themselves into two great processions. He sees them traveling by just two roads. One of these is a broad road; the other is narrow. And there is no third road in between. That is, every man is a pilgrim, and is traveling either by the broad way or by the narrow.

Then, the text is forbidding, in the second place, because it commends the narrow way. Now, "narrow" is an offensive word. Frankly, we do not like it. It connotes that which repels. It suggests the unpleasant. It smacks of the distasteful. When we hear it we think of the dwarfed mind; we think of the stunted soul; we think of the blurred vision and the contracted view. We are reminded of the provincial whose interests and whose sympathies are bounded by his own yard fence. We think of the sectarian who has a corner on the Infinite, and the greater part of whose religious joy grows out of his conviction that his brother is wrong rather than that he himself is right. We do not admire narrow folks. We do not wish to be narrow ourselves. Yet in the face of this we hear Jesus saying: "Enter by the narrow gate."

II

Why are we to enter by the narrow gate? It is surely not because it is easier to travel the narrow way than it is to travel the broad. Even if such were the case, it is well to remember that Jesus never once appealed to our love of ease in his efforts to win our loyalty. He frankly calls upon us to face the fact that to be a follower of him involves difficulties. He tells us that to walk with him is expensive, that it costs to enter in at the strait gate and to follow the narrow way. This is true because, the gate being narrow, we cannot enter it so easily as we can the wide gate. We can enter the wide gate and carry with us all our sins, all our selfishness, all our prejudices and hates and lusts. But to enter the narrow gate is exacting. To enter it, much must be left behind.

We must leave all our sins. We must renounce every wrong attitude. We must be ready to give up, not only every known wrong, but every practice that is questionable. We must renounce our very selves. "For if any man will come after me, let him deny himself." Then, too, if we enter by this gate we must load ourselves with certain very definite obligations. We must become a bearer of burdens. We must become our brother's keeper. Our right to do as we please must be utterly renounced. We must take our place among those whose lives have certain limitations. Ours must be lives that are fenced in with such fences as "I ought" and "I must."

If we are to enter by the narrow gate and walk the narrow road, we must renounce the privilege of walking with the majority. That is not easy for most of us. We love the crowd. We love to feel that the multitude is on our side. But Jesus very openly declares that those who travel the narrow way walk with the few, not with the many. This was surely overwhelmingly true when Jesus was here. It is true even to this day, though those who walk the narrow road have vastly increased. But, even yet, he who chooses the narrow way must be willing to travel with the few. We must even be willing, if the need arises, to walk alone.

Why, then, are we urged to choose a road that is narrow and difficult? We are so urged because it leads to a worth-while goal. The first concern of every traveler is his destination. It is surely not enough to make speed. Rapid progress is worse than nothing unless it be in the right direction. The home of my boyhood was a most inaccessible place. But, when I was away at school, and the session was over, I did not go to the railroad station and ask for a ticket on the most popular train leaving the city. I asked for a ticket on the train that went toward my home. When I had gone as far as possible on the train, I had to travel over a horrible dirt road. But I faced all the difficulties involved simply because the road, in spite of its hindrances, led home. I was willing to travel the road, not because it was easy, but because it brought me to the goal of my desires.

"Enter ye in at the strait gate." Why? "Because strait is the gate, and narrow is the way, which leadeth unto life." It is worth while to travel the narrow road because by so doing one finds life. And by life here Jesus does not mean mere existence, but right existence, existence in fellowship with himself. And by destruction, which he tells us is the goal of the broad road, he does not mean extinction. He means rather the ruin that of necessity overtakes the soul that is separated from God. The narrow road leads to life, and it is the only road that does. Therefore with wisdom he urges all of us to make it our choice.

III

But why is the road to life narrow? In a God-ordered world we should expect that it would be the opposite. We feel that the way to death should be a narrow and difficult road, but that the road to life should be broad and easy. Why is not this the case? Why, at least, is not the way of life as broad as the way of death? In seeking an answer to these questions we may at least be sure of this: The way of life is certainly not narrow because God arbitrarily decreed that it should be so. It is true that Jesus declares that the way is narrow. But his saying so does not make it narrow. But knowing it to be narrow, he, in his mercy, tells us the truth about it. I used to have an arithmetic that declared emphatically that three times three is nine. But the fact that this book made such a declaration did not cause such result. Three times three is nine whether any book says so or not. And the way to life is narrow whether the fact is ever put into words or not. It is narrow in the nature of things. In fact, the road to every goal is a narrow road.

Did you ever go bird-hunting? If so, I guarantee that your first experience was a bit after this fashion: The dog found a covey of quails and flushed them. Your friend picked out a single bird and brought it down. You fired at the whole covey and killed

THE WAY OF LIFE

nothing. This kept up till your friend said: "Don't shoot at the whole twenty; shoot at one." And what did he mean by this? If one is to hunt birds, narrow is the way. There are ten thousand ways that a hunter may miss the mark. There is only one way that he can hit it.

There is a magnificent skyscaper being built in our city. Do you suppose that the architect who planned this building went about the task in a careless and slipshod manner? Did he draw all sorts of pictures and make numerous blue prints just as the mood of the moment led him, without any regard to whether they were accurate or not? No, he found the way exceedingly narrow. His drawings and his calculations could not be made at random. They could not be only approximately correct, they had to be exactly correct. And the contractor who is undertaking to make the dream of the architect into a reality is also having to travel a narrow road. He cannot follow any set of blue prints that chances to fall into his hands. He is shut up to only one. No more can he presume to change those drawn by the architect according as the whim strikes him. He must build exactly as planned. Truly, "narrow is the way."

Every evening a train leaves our city for New York. Under what conditions can that train hope to make a successful journey? What instructions shall we give? Just this: "Narrow is the way." If that train will not follow the narrow way, it becomes a wreck. A ship is leaving New York for Europe.

What shall we say to this great vessel? "Narrow is the way." For it does not sail for the whole continent of Europe; it sails for one little speck upon the map. If it fails to do so, if it will not follow the narrow way, it becomes derelict.

And what shall we say to the man who would be a scientist? This same forbidding word: "Narrow is the way." Certainly this was the experience of Charles Darwin. He found the road of the scientist most narrow. It was so narrow that he lost his taste for music. It was so narrow that he lost his taste for poetry. It was so narrow that his mind became a mere machine, as he himself says, for grinding out general laws from certain known facts. Edison has also found the way narrow. He has found it so narrow that, in spite of his vast ability, he has missed, I fear, the very finest that life has to offer.

The same is true in the realm of literature, of art, and of music. The writer of great prose must walk a narrow way. The writer of great poetry must travel one that is more narrow still. The painter cannot handle his brush carelessly and sleepily and stupidly. If he ever succeeds in splashing a great dream upon the canvas, he must travel a narrow road. And the great musician also finds himself shut up to the same necessity. For all these, "Narrow is the way." The broad road is always at hand with its greater throngs and its easier travel, but it fails to lead to the desired goal.

Here is a young couple that has decided to share

life with each other in the marriage relationship. It is a high adventure, full of possible romance and poetry. How may they hope to succeed? How may they find the fullest and deepest joy? How shall we instruct them? We must tell them that narrow is the way. "John, wilt thou have Mary to thy wedded wife, to live together after God's ordinance in the holy estate of matrimony? Wilt thou love her, comfort her, honor and keep her, in sickness and in health; and forsaking all other, keep thee only unto her, so long as ye both shall live?" "It is a narrow way, indeed!" you say. "Yes, but it is the only way that leads to a successful wedded life. All other roads end in tragic failure."

Therefore we need not be surprised nor resentful when Jesus tells us that the way that leads to life is narrow. He himself found it so. He is speaking out of his own experience. He gave himself to one insignificant country at the back side of civilization. He never passed beyond its boundaries into the really great nations of the world. He gave himself mainly to one little handful of men, not one of whom counted for much until he found him. He was shut in by tremendous convictions. There were certain things that he felt he must do. He had a work to accomplish from which he could not turn aside. His way was so narrow that when it ran up against a cross there was not room for him to pass round that cross. He had to hang upon it. Truly his was a narrow road, and invites you and me to follow in his steps.

IV

But while the way to life is narrow and the way to death is broad, we are not to overestimate either the narrowness of the one or the breadth of the other. The way of life is narrow, yet it is broad enough to meet all our needs.

1. It is wide enough to accommodate all who are willing to travel it. In spite of the narrowness of the gate, everybody may pass through that gate who is willing to pay the price. When Jesus was dying, a highwayman hung at his side. There was blood on this man's hands. He had an evil and ugly past. But in his hour of death he turned to the dying Christ at his side and said: "Lord, remember me when thou comest into thy kingdom." And the narrow gate proved to be amply wide for him to enter, and he found himself traveling the road that leads to life.

When the prodigal came back, he had no good word to say for himself. He knew he had no right to come. He only hoped that by being very humble and very penitent he might find a place in the servants' quarters. He would at least go and knock at the door and ask for an interview. And what was the result? Did the father look down from some upper window and ask what he had done with his money, where and how he had squandered his moral and spiritual wealth? Did he say, "O yes, I knew you would come trekking home when you had spent your all and had nowhere else to go"? No, his father rather ran to meet him and gave him a welcome home. For, though the gate is narrow, it is yet wide enough, I repeat, to admit any who is willing to enter.

2. This road is wide enough for us to walk arm in arm with Christ. Such a road may be narrow, but it is none too narrow. The broad road, with all its breadth, is not wide enough for that. It is said of the prodigal that he gathered all together and took his journey into a far country. But there were some treasures that he did not take with him. There were many priceless things that he was compelled to leave behind. He could not take his old home with him. He could not take his father. He could not take his faith. He could not take God. The road to death is broad, but it is not broad enough for one to walk it in the fellowship of Jesus Christ.

3. Then, this narrow road is wide enough to permit all of us to come to our best and to realize our highest possibilities. For the fact that the way is narrow does not mean that those who walk it must themselves be narrow. The opposite is true. It is as we travel the narrow way that we ourselves become broad. Real Christians are never narrow. They cannot be. This is true because they share in the nature of Christ. And how broad is he! The breadth of Jesus is the breadth of the Infinite.

To walk with Christ in the narrow way is to become broad in our sympathies. How boundless was the sympathy of Christ! It bridged all chasms. It broke through all sundering barriers. It went out to good and bad, to far and near, to wise and foolish, to those who loved him and to those who hated him. It took in the whole world. And a kindred breadth of sympathy he gives to those who know him. How narrow was John when Jesus found him! How narrow he was even during the early days of his discipleship! He was eager to burn down a little Samaritan village that had refused his Master hospitality. He pridefully sought to prevent a servant of God from doing good because he did not serve in just the same manner as himself. But how big he became as he traveled with Jesus in the narrow way! Of Christ's fullness he received. Therefore, before he reached the end of his journey, he had the weight of a world's need upon his heart.

As we walk the narrow way we become broad in our purposes. Here is Jesus at prayer. And what a narrow prayer he is offering! "I pray not for the world, but for them whom thou hast given me." Then he broadens out a bit: "Neither pray I for these alone, but for them also who shall believe on me through their word." That is better. It was then that he called your name and mine, if we are believers. But we feel that the prayer is still too narrow till we come to this thrilling word: "That the world may know that thou hast sent me." The purposes of Jesus take in the whole world. He is seeking to establish his reign over all the earth. He never will and never can be satisfied with anything less than the complete conquest of the world. And those who walk with him in the narrow way are privileged to share his vast dreams and work with him in his great enterprise. The followers of the narrow way are, therefore, broad in their purposes.

Those who walk the narrow way are broad in their hopes. All who journey by the broad road have hopes that are of necessity very small and very limited. They can stretch but a little way into the future. They bring but little joy while they last and are soon blighted by the biting frosts of death. All of them are bounded by the grave. But our hopes stretch away into the infinite eternities. They are so big and broad that they enable us to face all life's tragedies with steady eyes and quiet hearts. They enable us to laugh at death and the grave in the full assurance that these can work us no harm, since we are the sons of God and are on our way to be like him when we shall see him as he is.

Now, because the narrow road leads to life abundant in this present world, and because it leads to an ever fuller life in the eternal to-morrow, I have great boldness in inviting you to enter by the narrow gate. Remember, you are going to travel one way or the other. You cannot in the nature of the case walk both roads. As you came to church to-night, you came either by the broad road or by the narrow. As you go home, I do not know what street you will travel, but I do know that you will go either by the broad road or by the narrow. I know also that the road you travel determines your goal.

As there are only two roads, so there are only two goals, only two destinations. One is Life, the other is Death. Therefore, on the authority of my Lord, I am placing before you at this moment Life and Death. May we all have the wisdom and the courage to make choice of Life!

XVII

THE TWO BUILDERS

Matthew 7: 24-27

"Therefore whosoever heareth these sayings of mine, and doeth them, I will liken him unto a wise man which built his house upon a rock: and the rain descended, and the floods came, and the winds blew, and beat upon that house; and it fell not: for it was founded upon a rock. And every one that heareth these sayings of mine, and doeth them not, shall be likened unto a foolish man, which built his house upon the sand: and the rain descended, and the floods came, and the winds blew, and beat upon that house; and it fell: and great was the fall of it."

THIS parable marks the close of Matthew's version of the Sermon on the Mount. Jesus has been preaching to a vast and interested multitude. They have listened to him with mingled amazement and gladness. In conclusion he tells them, as he tells us, that it is not enough to listen, even though we listen with reverent approval. It is not enough to listen, even though we listen with keen appreciation and with emotions deeply stirred. If our listening is to be of any worth, it must lead to action. We must not only hear, we must obey. It was to enforce this truth that Jesus told the story of the two builders whose buildings were tested by the storm.

I

The first fact that Jesus brings home to our hearts in this story is that all who hear are builders. Of course we build, whether we hear or not; but it is to the hearers that he is confining himself in this parable. All who hear, he tells us, are builders. These builders he divides into two classes. There are the wise builders, and there are the foolish. Jesus, as we have noticed before, is constantly dividing folks into two groups. There are those who have the wedding garment, and those who do not. There are those who travel the broad way, and those who travel the narrow. There are those who are spiritually alive, and those who are spiritually dead. We of to-day do not relish such divisions. But the fact remains that Jesus makes them, and makes them constantly.

Now, the wise man is a builder. He is constructing something. He is building his own character. He is building his soul-home. He is building the temple in which he is to spend eternity. The same is equally true of the foolish man. He, too, is building. He, too, is constructing the temple or the hovel or the sty in which he is to spend eternity. Both alike are builders.

This is true of all of us. We are building all the time, whether wisely or foolishly. We are building by everything that we do. We are building by every thought that we think. We are building by every word that we speak, every dream that we

THE TWO BUILDERS 219

dream, every picture that we hang upon the walls of our imagination, every ambition that we cherish. All these go to make up the material that enters into the structure that we are building for the ages.

Some of us are putting some shoddy stuff into our buildings. We are putting material that cannot stand the test of the storm. That oath that you swore, that thoughtless blasphemy that you flung from your lips, that was poor material. That foul story that you told, that unclean thing that you did, that, too, was shoddy. That time that you ran with the multitude to do evil out of sheer cowardice; that time when you remained silent when you should have spoken—that, too, was poor stuff to put into your soul temple. That time you clutched your money in the presence of a pressing need; that time you passed by on the other side when a wounded life was calling to you—that also was shoddy. The fact that you are standing to-day, though a member of the Church, with your membership hidden away in the country or buried in your trunk, trying to play the neutral when God is needing soldiers—that means that you are putting some very flimsy stuff into your building.

Then some are building stanchly and beautifully. That was fine material that the widow put into her building when she threw in her two mites for love's sake. That was fine material that Daniel put into his soul palace when he purposed in his heart that he would not defile himself. That was rugged and substantial stuff that Joseph used when he fled his temptation, even though his escape cost him the horrors of a dungeon. That is fine material you are using as you walk life's common ways in loving loyalty to your duty as God gives you to see your duty.

But whether we are building wisely or foolishly, we are all building. Nor are our lives fragmentary things. They are not so much brick and lumber and mortar and nails flung down in confusion. Every life is a whole, with certain definite moral characteristics. For instance, when the Old Testament tells us that a certain king did evil in the sight of the Lord, that does not mean that every act of his life was necessarily wicked. It means only that the man was inwardly evil and that, therefore, the prevailing tone of his life was of the same character. Likewise, when it says of another that he did that which was right in the sight of the Lord, this does not mean that every act of his life was perfect, but that its prevailing tone, its moral characteristic was upright and pure. But whether wisely or foolishly, we are all building.

II

The second fact that our Lord brings to our attention is this, that the buildings that we are constructing, the characters we are making are going to be tested. For this reason we are not to build for fair weather only. We must build with a view to hours of crises. We must build with a view to

THE TWO BUILDERS 221

times of tempest. For, sooner or later, to all the testing comes. Upon you, and you, and you some day the storm will surely break.

This is the case whether we build wisely or foolishly. The building of the foolish man is going to be tested, but the building of the wise man is going to be tested too. God does not coddle his saints. He does not protect them from the stress and strain of life. He never promises them exemption from conflict. Our Lord prays for us, but he never prays that we may dodge the storm and have an easy time. "I pray not that thou shouldest take them out of the world, but that thou shouldest keep them from the evil." He means for us not to flee the tempest, but to face it and defy it. For to all the storm must come.

We realize the fact of the coming storm in the making of our material structures. We do not want a garment that will spot and fade the moment a drop of water touches it. We seek to have those that will retain their shape and color. When I was a boy, seersucker suits were sometimes worn in summer. But woe unto the man that was overtaken by a rain! By the time he got dry his sleeves were to his elbows and his trousers to his knees. The ship that is constructed to sail only upon a glassy sea and under blue skies will not do for oceans like ours, where the heavens so often become black and where the seas are so often whipped by the tempest. Our bridges must be able to sustain more than their own weight. They must stand heavy tests. They must be built with a view to a city's traffic. In the building of our houses, whether private or public, we must take the tempest into consideration. To fail to do so would mean disaster.

While I was pastor in Washington a few years ago there came a terrific snowstorm. For more than thirty-six hours the snow fell till it lay deep on the earth and upon the roofs of the houses. There was a theater in that city that was a thing of beauty, but the architect had only sunny days in his eye when he planned it. He foolishly built without due regard to the coming storm. Therefore, when the snow lay some thirty inches deep upon it, the strain was too great. The roof crashed, and more than one hundred lives were lost in the disaster.

Now, Christ tells us frankly that the test is coming to ourselves. Upon some here present heavy storms have already broken. You are in God's house even now having by his grace come bravely through more than one trying tempest. Others of you have seen your lives crash in ruins. For, while there are some who have storm-proof religion, there are others whose religion is a plaything of the winds. The rude fists of the tempest dash it ruthlessly aside. But to all the storm comes. Just when it is coming we do not know. It may be to-day; it may be to-morrow. Just how it is coming we do not know. It does not come to all alike.

1. Sometimes the storm breaks upon us in the guise of a great temptation. We are brought suddenly face to face with an inducement to evil that

we feel, if we accept, must line our pathway with roses. If we refuse, life will become a desert. A successful young banker said to me the other day, very seriously and very earnestly: "The most persistent petition in my prayer is this: 'Lead us not into temptation.'" It is a wise prayer. We need to pray it, every one of us; for any hour our crisis may be upon us. Any hour we may be overwhelmed if He does not help us weather the gale.

2. The storm may come in the guise of some bitter personal loss. One day out of the blue the news may come that you have lost every penny that you possessed; that from plenty you have been reduced to poverty; that the wolf is now howling at your very door. Or, worse still, it may be some bitter personal loss, the slipping out of your home of a loved one dearer to you than life. It may mean the sundering of ties most tender and binding. I wonder, when the storm comes, if you will be able to say with the stanch faith of Job: "The Lord gave, and the Lord hath taken away: blessed be the name of the Lord."

Or, what is even harder to bear, if we read Job's record aright, there may come to you the complete loss of health. There may come the persistent gnawing of physical pain. Sentence of death may be passed upon you weary months before its execution. You may be called on to suffer and to suffer long. Torture may sit astride your chest and clutch at your throat and lay its burning hands so heavily upon your lips that at times you cannot pray. When that terrible storm comes, I wonder if you can stand up against it bravely enough to say: "Though he slay me, yet will I trust him."

3. Then the storm may be of a different character. Instead of blowing away your treasure, it may bring it in larger abundance. When the Israelites were in the wilderness, there came to them a time of storm. But it blew nothing away. It brought them wealth. They were half buried in delicious quails. But those days of luxury were by no means their best days. They became days of pestilence and plague. These people could not endure prosperity. The place of their enrichment became a graveyard. The name of it signifies the "graves of lust." They were made to realize the tragic fact that there is a destruction that wasteth at noonday.

It is such a tempest that constitutes one of the chief dangers of our land to-day. Our spiritual progress lags so far behind our material progress. We are rich in things, but often deadly poor in the wealth that outlasts the ages. It is hard to face a tempest of adversity. It is harder still to stand against an avalanche of prosperity. As the Roman girl who promised to lead an invading army into her city if each soldier would give her the bracelet from his own arm was crushed under the weight of her own wealth, so many a one is crushed to-day. Happy is the man who lives in the consciousness of the fact that his life consisteth not in the abundance of the things that he possesseth.

4. Finally, to every one of us is coming the test of the judgment. This is true of those who build

THE TWO BUILDERS

wisely. It is true of those who build foolishly. Every one of us is on the road to the hour of testing. That is as certain as the fact of life. It is as certain as the fact of death. It is as certain as the fact of God. "Every man must give an account of himself to God. . . . For we must all stand before the judgment seat of Christ. . . . For it is appointed unto man once to die, but after this the judgment."

How supremely important, therefore, that we should build wisely and well, for every man's building is going to be tested!

> "Build thee more stately mansions, O my soul,
> As the swift seasons roll.
> Leave thy low-vaulted past,
> Let each new temple, nobler than the last,
> Shut thee from heaven with a dome more vast,
> Till thou at length art free,
> Leaving thine outgrown shell by life's unresting sea."

III

The final fact that our Lord brings before us is that the issues of the testing are not going to be the same for all.

1. Some are not going to be able to stand the test. This is true of all whose lives are not founded on Himself and his teaching. What a bold and daring declaration! Yet he makes it, and makes it without the slightest flinching. He makes it without the least modification. "If you do not build on me," he says frankly, "your house will not stand. One day the tempest will swoop down upon it and tear it

to fragments. One day there will be a crash, then shreds of wreckage upon the raging waters, and the ruin will be complete." "For other foundation can no man lay than that is laid, which is Jesus Christ."

2. But there are those, thank God, that are going to pass through the testing without loss. There are those that are going to outride all storms. There are those that are going to weather all gales. This is true of all who have builded their lives upon Jesus Christ. For such a life it is going to be written in time, and it is going to be written in eternity: "It fell not." "He shall be like a tree planted by rivers of water." He remains steadfast. He is unhurt amidst the crash of tempests and the wreck of worlds. "For the world passeth away, and the lust thereof; but he that doeth the will of God abideth forever." Such are the stupendous claims of Jesus, and these high claims have been vindicated countless millions of times. Lives builded on him really do stand the test.

A few years ago a mission worker who was a beautiful saint went to comfort a friend who had lost a wife. If this friend was a Christian at all, he was only nominally so. The minister spoke to him of the consolations of the gospel. But the bereaved man turned on him bitterly and said: "Have you ever lost your wife?" The preacher answered in the negative. "Well," said the other impatiently, "you don't know what you are talking about. Wait till you have a sorrow like mine and see if your Christ can meet the test."

THE TWO BUILDERS

The preacher went away with a sense of failure. But the testing time was closer to him, too, than he dreamed. Suddenly, without the slightest warning, the news came that his brilliant and gifted wife had been killed in a railroad accident. The remains were brought to the city and taken to the mission hall. This grief-stricken husband stood by the coffin of his wife to speak. He said: "Some six months ago I tried to comfort a bereaved husband, but I failed. He said I did not know what I was talking about. Is he here?" And the man stood up. The preacher then continued: "My friend, I know to-day. I am in the midst of a sorrow like your sorrow, and I want to tell you that, while my heart is bleeding and broken, I find His grace sufficient. I find that his hand holds me and steadies me. I find that my skies are as bright as the promises of God, and that underneath are the Everlasting Arms." May you find your foundation so secure when you come to your testing! If you do, you must build upon the Rock of Ages.